Previous books by Dr. Alan Cooper, DC

Available Online

I, Cancer: The Semi-Buddhist Answer to
Dancing with Cancer ... You Lead

Available only at miraclestruggle@gmail.com

Panda: The Guru Weeps

The Agony of Victory, The Ecstasy of Defeat

Spiritual Alchemy: The Shy Messiah

SUBTRACTING INSULT FROM INJURY

A Buddheo-Christian Art of Transmuting Pain

DR. ALAN COOPER D.C.

The cover art is a painting by Ron Cooper (no relation) entitled *Tidal Dissipation.* See his work at roncooperart.com

Balboa Press books may be ordered through booksellers or by contacting:

Balboa Press
A Division of Hay House
1663 Liberty Drive
Bloomington, IN 47403
www.balboapress.com
1 (877) 407-4847

Print information available on the last page.

ISBN: 978-1-5043-9723-0 (sc)
ISBN: 978-1-5043-9722-3 (hc)
ISBN: 978-1-5043-9724-7 (e)

Library of Congress Control Number: 2018901308

Balboa Press rev. date: 02/26/2018

I sincerely dedicate this book to you, the reader. If I have toiled over the seeds of ideas contained within, and they take no purchase in the seeking soil of your souls, I will be a fallow farmer indeed. I thus extend gratitude that you might stretch your inquisitiveness to ponder the atypical view of human pain here posed. Only through you, might the quantum eye sunder mystery's veil.

Contents

Acknowledgements

At a critical juncture of this creation, Jade Colleen Webb and her loving editorial verve inhaled a new breath into a somewhat hypoxic incarnation of this book. Thank you, kind friend. Thank you.

A few Thanksgivings ago my friend Dr. Amy Maher, Medical Doctor and Chronic Pain Specialist, called and invited me for tea and a talk. Over that steaming brew days later, the seeds of this creation were sown. Though our original vision to write the book together morphed into my solo flight, (Amy having a young child to raise and a busy Medical practice,) she is indeed the beloved mama of this endeavor.

To Neta, Jeta, Jana, Sevdije, Ryve, Sheqerie, Fatos, and all those Kosovars who meet me in that place far beyond words: *dashuri ime per juve eshte pakufizur.*

To Casey, Sally, Katie, Sophie, Will, Cloee, Cicily, Ariel, and Abel, the nine giant Cooper trees who inhabit the forest in which I was born. Your oxygen fills my lungs, and I dedicate my capacity to still dream to you all.

To Helen Quail, my Beauty—you've taken me out onto life's sacred dance floor. Like a master Geppetto, the way you navigate love deep in the body and soul has helped turn my Pinocchio from a puppet into a real man. Your depths are in my vision.

Preface

Imagine Life's Unequalled

"No Pain, No Gain"

What if, without exaggeration,

every anguish every human
has ever or will ever endure
unfalteringly cultivates the
decisive, poignant dynamic
of the Infinite Design?

A divine intention to transform
heavy into heaven; an alchemic
disburdening, lightning, and

soothing of the agonizingly dense pre-Big Bang Primordial Compression of dark matter, black holes, and dark energy!

Astrophysicists have conclusively established that once upon the timeless place, before the big bang was even a twinkle in the infinite eye, all that existed was constrained into an unfathomably solitary, dense black hole-like singularity. Unitary and imploding as it was, they have aptly baptized it the *Primordial Compression*.

As such, it initially harbored seeds of but a single primal sensation: quintessentially dense, contracting, and penetratingly gravitational. If we were to anthropomorphize, it is fair to say we might dare christen the experiential perception of this feeling, ***pain***.

After eons of unconditional immobility, following a fundamental law of physics, there was an equal and opposite reaction to the ostensibly never-ending dark contraction. Let there be light! A hallowed birth! A big bang!

The here-to-fore eternal black hole ruptured into trillions of smaller particles of dark matter and energy. With many of them wedded to nascent bits of the exploding expansiveness we know as *Light*, the pain had been divided into exponentially more manageable, healable, and illumined increments.

That which we call God, Goddess, the Infinite, or Cosmic Consciousness had hatched a sacred curative design. In this burgeoning strategy, many of these newly expanding shards of dark matter and energy ultimately came to rest in the divine creation of human beings. Replete with a qualified modicum of God's capacity for insight and expansive soothing, each of these souls was requisitioned to thus alchemically lighten an allocated portion of the original dense dark primordial pain.

As 'the plan' entailed, each individual's allotment of primordial compression emerged from their gut/soul, in karmic unconscious, time-encrypted rhythms. These increments of dark matter and energy (*dukkha*) were thus to be healed through daily living, loving, art, work, and our noble quests to make life vibrant and meaningful. A cosmic miracle was afoot, except …

As astronomers note, our universe consists of roughly ninety percent dark matter and dark energy and but ten percent our cherished light and visible matter. Accordingly, when massive waves of primordial compression first emerged to be rehabilitated through the soul portals of the earliest prototypical human beings, these ultra-dense sensations predominantly overwhelmed the relatively limited capacity of the skimpy light. Though God had done the best He initially could, the human contraption was by nature impeccably flawed, and the precarious plan staggered and faltered. Infinite consciousness deemed that "knowing what the gods know" of the daunting task of healing something nine times bigger than light was turning out to be a fruit too wretched to bear.

And so it was, alack and alas, with a tad of tinkering and celestial sleight of hand, that *ego* was thus conceived to play a shell game with the dark, heavy reality. The tree of knowledge was forbidden, and humans were redesigned with Alice in Wonderland trapdoors to a house of mirrors, in the place called Egoville. Like a modern-day game of laser tag, in Egoville the light in a human soul no longer was compelled to drearily shine on its own voluminous mountain of darkness. Instead, it shot its beams outward at one another, and by cognizance of the shafts of light that returned in reaction, an ego initiated the generating of an autobiography. Immersed in this fresh holographic potpourri of imagery, a human was suddenly at liberty to behold oneself as an amalgamation of all the light beam impressions others shot their way. With beams bouncing off the walls of our minds and hearts, it was cool to forget the painful reality of our origin and the dispiriting task we had been created to carry out. By moving the seat of consciousness out of the gut/soul and into the mind/ego, light could thoroughly preoccupy itself with juicy skullduggery and illusory points of view. With a colossal sigh of relief, humankind dug in for the long journey, opinions proving to be much more palatable than the nuisance of cumbersome energy and feelings. With these capricious deliberations intact, egoistic ignorance was institutionally cast in stone, as bliss.

But like all potent intoxicants, the bliss was fleeting. As history has appallingly exposed, to keep the laser tag adequately powerful, the dominant ego matrix has had to remain fervent in veiling the truth. It accomplishes this by pigeonholing all emergent sensations of primordial compression into dominions of failure, vengeance, and tragedy. We were and are still therefore reduced to living in a near-constant state of adding insults to injuries. We are beholden to fallaciously categorize every opportunity our earmarked portion of density arises to be mended, as sad, victim-tainted, presumably needless and avoidable occurrences.

As our relatively unsophisticated minds clumsily trample on the delicate enigma that is at the roots of the forbidden tree of knowledge, we live immersed in the childlike shelter of dualistic good and bad. If something we deem as bad happens, we wholeheartedly ascribe goodness as its implicit opposite antidote. Assessed as such, inquiry dies. The gifts of complexity and nuance are lost. The good guys will beat the bad guys. Those we perceive to be misbehaving will eventually comprehend our martyred pleas and listen to our self-righteous complaints about their malfeasance. And above all, the good God will wipe away the pesky bad parts of humanity. "Daddy, save us. Destroy the bad guys (and win me the lottery while you're at it if you have a sec)" And since the ego exclusively communicates in this Morse code of good-good-bad-good-bad-bad, virtually every pain is, by nature, deemed dangerous. A punch-drunk boxer bobbing and weaving and having been created *solely* to hide the adversity of the truth, the ego flourishes by vilifying that and those it deems to be the cause of our pains. And when the weight of primal density invariably breaks through the egoistic dam and floods us despite our best efforts, we castigate ourselves as being beneath contempt. "Woe is me; I am far too feeble and frail to resist the evil ones."

Then our never-say-die, fastidious egos redouble their exertions and fashion phantasmagorical forts around our beleaguered souls. Fort Alan, for instance, is fortified with the fortitude to fend off anyone from transgressing against me, like my Johnny on the spot ego insists I was unjustly injured as a child. These forts we facilitate in perpetuity take an overabundance of our precious oomph to maintain. The energy existing in living cells is physiologically equipped to do but one of two things. It will either protect an organism or buttress it in its flourishing. It lacks the capacity to do both simultaneously. Programmed then in our defensive fort mode, we thoroughly strip ourselves of the very dynamism we might otherwise use to thrive.

The fort not only wastes valuable vivacity in this fool's errand, but it also presupposes tacit wisdom in our issues, victimization, resentment, triggers, and self-protection. Thus, even spiritually evolving people too often compartmentalize their pains into victim-laden jargon, wisdom-less crucibles held outside their otherwise inherent knowing. But what is worse, the forts we have manufactured around our permeable, gorgeously vulnerable souls, deny us the greatest accolade we so richly deserve.

We are irrefutably among the most marvelous creations of the universe, veritable healing machines. Made in the image of God or universal intelligence, we are built to process dense dark matter and dark energy into grace. This book, *Subtracting Insult from Injury,* is a voyage beginning in the fleeting intoxicating lies and degradation of ego-bliss. If we are brave enough, it will take us through the momentary sobering of forbidden truth, all the way to the freedom to know unambiguously the cosmic motive behind all our pain and the grace we spontaneously produce through countenancing it. Thus set free, we can know why life created us, and behold the flood of a fast-approaching miracle of mystical resolution.

Still, if "ignorance is bliss" and "the truth hurts," it would appear to be a fool's errand for me to imply to you that humanity will be better off grasping the cosmos' heavier, darker realism. Yet because "the truth sets us free," I will gamble that our species will ultimately be better served *to know what the gods know.* And yes, I confess that after thirty-six years of beating this inquiry to a veritable pulp, I respectfully believe and offer that some of the answers have strode from behind the veil, and under duress, revealed a few delectable canapés of its secret to me.

An old Irish proverb proclaims: "In our togetherness, castles are built." If you, my dear reader, and I, are to build a bonny bastion of fruitfulness together on the fertile side of this literary drawbridge, it's best to establish what we are each seeking. As for me, I have written this book in reaction to what I perceive as two cavernous voids. The first concerns a paucity of wisdom regarding the current scourge of deaths from medically prescribed opioids. The second encompasses the reflexive way most of us routinely react to our emotional and physical pains with fear, stress, anger, defeat, guilt and blame. From garden-variety temper tantrums to school shootings to hostility- engorged divorces to ethnic cleansings, I believe that the counterproductive turbulent neurotransmitters that flood our bodies in reaction to deep discomfort could all be palliated by a new wisdom.

And what of you, what are your longings? If the castle you

aspire to is quite clear-cut, you may not want or need to read all of my philosophical chapters. If you are a Medical Practitioner yearning for a breath of new air regarding your over-medicated chronic pain patients, Chapter 3 alone might satiate you. If you are a chronic pain sufferer, Chapters 4 and 5 are designed for you. If your pains are more emotional and mental, Chapters 6 and 7 were written for you. If you struggle with romantic relationships, Chapter 8 addresses this problem. If you are a woman suffering from misogyny and virulent patriarchy, I trust Chapters 10 and 11 could ease you some. And, if your children feel disconnected and self-centered, Chapter 16 might help.

As to the rest of the book, it is a philosophical trek into the cosmic rationality and utility of human pain. If your net is wide and your curiosity deep as the darkest ocean, perhaps the challenge of these new abstractions will feed you. If my scratching beneath the surface occasionally strikes you as repetitive and long-winded, I apologize. I felt the need to counter our collective programmed assumptions about pain by repeatedly driving home a few of my salient beliefs. For my money, the book is occasionally a bit dense, so proceed at your own gentle pace. And thank you big time for meeting me out in our castle in the quantum field, where new ideas are every now and again fertilized in the eyes of the beholder.

Introduction

Doubtless, sometime, somewhere, someone bade you that bushel-full of judicious, offhandedly rhetorical advice to "stop adding insult to injury." So darn sorry, but *news flash*: it's abundantly too late! You have been utterly swallowed by a lifetime of self-incrimination, such that a mountain of insults now sits on your chest, biding its truculent time. Your psyche has been obstinately engaged in perpetuity, unwittingly drowning itself in a cesspool of self-slander robotically attached to every discomfort you undergo. After a lifetime of these semiconscious negative avowals, this deleterious verbiage is pathologically fastened like Velcro to your tender being. As if the egoistic mind would whine that it had missed its assigned duty otherwise, it jumps at the prospect of substantiating that virtually all pains are contemptible missteps, oversights, or cruelties. Although you are perchance just momentarily sad, vulnerable, anxious, or in physical pain, the ego has its act quite together, thank you. Handy as a whippersnapper, it quite succinctly reduces all the naturally complex convolutions of a human life down to some smarmy putdown of your being or others'. Like that bratty kid taunting you during recess back in the second grade, the intellect sneeringly anoints you a "loser, loser, loser." No, you are not allowed to merely experience disorientation, adrift on the sea of life for a day. Nor can you accept with benign equanimity an unknown sensation of physical discomfort that doesn't immediately have a box your mind can place it in. Your ego will resolutely frighten you or declare you to be a pathetic dud. Oh so many oodles of insults have been so sloppily slathered atop our naked souls that the self-slurs are bound to us like Siamese twins. And if something from the bowels of your being occasionally bloodcurdlingly cries out for mercy from the relentless barrage of self-incrimination, you'll merely take an ever-so-petite breather and insult another instead of yourself.

And then there is that molten gut domain, your id, where unfettered atmospheres sporadically manage to flood the banks of your socially correct superego. Oh, heaven forbid when that happens and you comport yourself in a way that rocks the big boat of societal normalcy. Delores the do-gooder superego, and Eddie the nag ego will castigate you up and down the block. They will broadcast these transgressions in neon and insult you to smithereens if you are foolhardy enough to attempt to live an unscripted, outside the box, gut-inspired, take no prisoners, life. From the ridiculous to the sublime, this philosophical enterprise will traverse the human mindscape from our chatterbox of staccato, daily, pint-sized self-insults all the way to the biblically ordained, species-wide forbidden fruit crash diet.

The negative spin ego adds as appendage upon virtually every discomfort is not only psychically maladaptive but somatically toxic to boot. Every morning that you arise with your natural pre-coffee existential weight of gravity and mild dread, and rather than parsing its substantial truths, you emblemize yourself "a *drag*," you initiate that day's vicious cycle. Each time you nonchalantly utter, "I must have slept wrong" as explanation for some morning misery, it needlessly denigrates your relationship with one of life's majestic, curative gifts. Every time you rationalize a twinge in your knee as, "I shouldn't have played so hard when I was young," you heartlessly disparage the wonders and freedoms of youth that life once openhandedly afforded you. And every time you add the obligatory, "I must have overdone it yesterday," to explain today's discomforts, you vilify the natural aging, still capacious capacities of your body and spirit. While these illustrations appear quite benign, they are strictly the tip of the iceberg. By the time the nitpicking negativity in response to pain has had its unquenchable way with you, your body has paid the dearest price. It has become inundated with adrenaline and its partner in crime, the stress hormone, cortisol. With these two chemicals boisterously steering the ship of fools, your health is being perilously squandered. Not only is pain relief suppressed by these bad-boy neural blues brothers, but a preponderance of immune activity as well.

As a hypnotherapist, I face our pervasive self-incrimination with an old-fashioned moral mini-tale. A woman climbing Mount Everest awakens in the dawn after an intense ascent the day before. Her knees and more are wailing; her freezing limbs are howling like hell. And yet, more than just her body rises with the sun above terra firma. From this higher otherworldly base camp, she does not denigrate her sleep, her childhood, nor her prior day's physical output. She adds no insults to her morning throbbing. She honors her own capacity to treat agony as an expected component of her trek. Moving forward in the face of her excruciating cells is her raison d'etre, the fundamental blooming of her inner flower. She automatically embraces whatever strength is left in her half-full cup and resolutely begins this day's heroic steps. Oh but allow me, dear reader, and I will exhibit to you that your time on this planet is wholly and unquestionably as gallant and laudable as hers.

As we endeavor to undo the hammering phenomenon of ego, we must concurrently advance a compassionate wisdom as to how and why it initially arose. There was an entirely pardonable blamelessness in the evolutionary necessity from whence our ego cacophony commenced. These reflexive, derogatory assessments once functioned as the mind's well-intentioned effort to nudge us toward survival by scratching the itch of the never-ending cup-half-empty conundrum: "Since I have this or that pain, what did I do *wrong*?" While answering this question once was the hallowed Darwinian feather in the human cap, this book will unequivocally exhibit to you that the up-to-date answer is, "Pain does not even minutely imply you have done anything wrong." No, today's insults are entwined as human nature only because their *absence* is utter anathema to our egos. And herein lies the epic human paradox. While adding insult to injury is both emotionally degrading and ruinous to our health, without these slanders, our ego-infused house of cards would crumble. The helium-like buoyancy of a self rises in proportion to its ardent stance that its principal purpose in life is to evade, sidestep, avoid, duck, elude, conquer, banish, skirt, blame, and outsmart pain. But if you feel at all ready to reconfigure the archetypal human computer program that presently demands your obeisance to a terribly outdated system, what's to follow should help.

I feel blessed to have worn a variety of hats in my lifetime, yet foremost I fancy myself a would-be philosopher. Much of this book then is a philosophical supposition, a hypothetical scrutiny of the roots of humanity's self-insulting, barely examined phenomena. Yet like any inherently contradictory enterprise, my thesis is that our consciousness has been evolutionarily adapted to hide the truth about pain from our orthodox thought patterns. How then can I expect you to even remotely embrace my radical premise? Perhaps your mind will be annoyed (or worse) at being challenged to shed its well-trodden version of deciphering your pains. Obviously you will then either kick this book into the trash-heap of misbegotten foolishness, or you will feel mayhap a gut curiosity that bids you towards the transmogrification of humanity's collective consciousness regarding pain.

My conviction is that humans are imbued with a singular and profound universal purpose, vis-à-vis the primordial pain. But for now, let's suspend our hubris for a heartbeat if we can. When a bear or an eagle or a whale or an elephant or a camel or an owl or a lion or an aardvark or an alligator experience pain, *they* react sanely. They find a safe, calm place to heal and be gently settled. This lack of hysteria fosters their natural restorative, pain-relieving endorphins and potent immune stimulators to be released into their bloodstreams. Without a pharmacy, a medical clinic, a hospital, a surgeon, or a psychotherapist, they instinctively lay still and rely on the unstinting rest, digest, and repair gifts of the parasympathetic nervous system.

They don't act in response to their anguishes by adding frightful, fuming, or subjugated judgments that propel bodies into the chemical mayhem of the sympathetic nervous system (fight, fright, and flight). The full thrust of this triple F neurological state was primordially ordained to be biologically reserved *only* for moments where life and death, abrupt and intense vigilance was mandatory for the continued existence of our species. In those instances, survival was dependent on suppressing the laid-back chemical parasympathetic endorphin cocktail the body releases to heal and alleviate pain. When danger was exigent, the body secreted chemicals that correctly blocked the blood from migrating inward to promote healing. Instead, it needed that blood broadcast outward to the limbs and mouth so we could scream and flee or fight.

Yet now, in this contemporary phase of human luxury, ninety-nine percent of the 3F *whirling dervish of danger dance* our minds and bodies still insistently perform is thoroughly useless and worse. Instead of natural pain relief and healing, humans fall predominantly into the vicious cycle of spooking ourselves in reaction to hurting. We are chemically suppressing our pain-relieving endorphins and other immune functions and consequently remaining in agony, which then spooks us ever the more. Animals may do some things to which we feel superior, but what they *don't* do is suppress healing and natural pain relief by adding, for example, any of the following insults to their injuries:

1. Crap always happens to me. God must hate me.
2. Nobody cares about me when I hurt this much.
3. I bet this pain in my armpit is cancer.
4. These pains will never go away. I'm just a loser.
5. I must have a big X on my back that says, "Hurt me."
6. I'm too weak to overcome this. I'm cursed.
7. My childhood was so hard that I'll never be happy.
8. I don't care that for 364 days nothing traumatic happened. The one day of trauma proves that my life will be screwed from now on.
9. That person is acting distant today. She must be angry at me.
10. I should have known better than to trust people.
11. This is too hard. I'll *never* be able to do this.
12. You don't really care. Nobody is there for me.
13. I'm just a drag. Everyone wishes I was dead.
14. Everyone else is normal. I'm the only one who is screwed.
15. It's my fault my parents are divorcing.
16. Of course this would happen to me just now.
17. I know this little cut will get infected.
18. Nobody appreciates my painful sacrifice.
19. I can't take it. I really can't.
20. "No pain, no gain," doesn't apply to me
21. If they force me into less pain meds, I can't make it.
22. If you knew everything that has happened to me …
23. Nobody loves me.

Or here are a few thick archetypal subconscious ones.

24. This pain in my leg is so bad. I know I'll be too messed up to run when the saber-toothed tiger tries to eat me.

25. I am utterly useless. I have so many aches and pains; I'm sure my tribe is getting ready to tie me to a tree so the animals will eat me. Then I won't be a drag anymore on the survivability of the "more fit" tribal members.

Or we throw a few blame bombs now and then.

26. If you weren't such an asshole, you'd never hurt me.
27. If you hadn't been arguing with me, I wouldn't have accidentally cut myself with that knife.
28. If I open up my old pains, I know you'll run away.
29. I gave you everything, and you gave me nothing.
30. Everyone sucks. I'm too good for these people.

Ad infinitum

Chapter 1

In the Beginning

Honestly friend, the only folks potentially bolstered by the observations to follow, might be those dear souls who heartrendingly hunger for a helping hand to elevate their rapport with life's myriad woes. So if your interplay with physical and emotional anguish is predicament-free, your temperament and body humming in unison like an impeccably oiled machine, then frankly, you're excused from this class. Go outside and have an extra period of gym. If you are even mildly intrigued, though, and choose to read on, I promise not to dance too roughly. I will nudge however, coercing you pointedly toward probing beneath your reflexive, damaging mental reactions to all discomfort. Anger, blame, guilt, defeat, hatred, and fear are all habitual emotional reactions we robotically embark on in response to hurting. And yet scratch beneath these emotive sinkholes and you will hear the insulting words that coerce the chemicals in your body to pour gasoline on even the tiniest of fires. It is these corrosive words that must be challenged (subtracted) before one can hope to alter the base passions that reign supreme over the angels of our better nature.

To begin to subtract insults from our injuries, we require as a prerequisite the configuration of a philosophical beachhead regarding the genesis of our self-slighting ritual. Our brains contain aspects of a reptilian mind, a mammalian mind, and of course, the latest and greatest Darwinian up-and-comer, the neo-cortex of the human mind. Though this book holds this third aspect, the humanoid mind, accountable for the insults we add to injury, this cognitive merry-go-round once singlehandedly secured our prolonged existence. Consequently, this 'survival of the fittest' domain of logical problem-solving was destined to become the poster child of simultaneous blessings and curses. In a prehistoric world where numerous species had various combinations of superior strength, more speed, or sharper teeth than us, our longevity one time teetered on an untenable abyss. Once upon this interminably overwhelming epoch, our upright descendants and their four-legged fellow earth dwellers all awoke at the crack of dawn, parched and craving water. After nodding "Good morning mate" to each other at the local watering hole, they gulped and guzzled, slurped, swigged, and swallowed heartily. Following a pleasant few minutes of drinking and discussing world affairs, a couple of otherwise swell saber-toothed tigers felt that familiar tug in their bellies. Grasping that it was time for morning repast, they gazed in gustatory ardor toward our two-legged ancestors. Before our descendants could sway the cats with, "Have you considered a vegan diet?" the humans became breakfast steak tartare for their famished feline friends.

It is a bit mind-jarring for our haughty species to picture being at that pathetic time and place, but the four-leggeds were plainly too damn fast and strong for us. So to counter this conspicuous disadvantage, nature responded by endowing us with a brand-spanking-new cerebral brainchild, and it was *thought*. Rather than being chow-chow-chow for Tony the Tiger every morning, Cavenaugh the Caveman became conscious that he could put off his visceral instinct to satiate his thirst. He began only to visit the pond after the annoying and impolite furry neighbors took their post-breakfast nap. Later still, he created primitive vessels to hold water, so when he awoke thirsty, he had liquid sustenance handy right in his cave. Time and again, in ways enormous and slight, the unyielding necessities of longevity would thrust their proverbial chins at him. And necessity, that mammy of all invention, would flood this new third mind with ways to effectively morph trepidation into survival-oriented, commonsensical responses. Yet before charming Cavenaugh was to be an up-and-coming suave man about town, he was more like Homer Simpson smacking himself in the head and screaming, "Doh!" every time he nearly lost his existence through thoughtless oversights. These self-proclamations of, "You idiot, you almost died!" were the first insults added to injury, and without them, we would not be the stately species we are today.

So the logic behind our dogged self-judgment might be just this pedestrian and obvious. Science Officer Spock could put the book down now, get back to his Star Trek duties, and be thoroughly satisfied with the itch of our question scratched. Yet along with this Darwinian cave-boy explanation for archetypal insults still painting today's coloring books of our lives, I have been stirred to unearth a far more unfathomable, primitive cosmic facet at play as well. Thus we will peel back the mirage of human ordinariness to a pre-human moment in celestial sub-history. There we will scrutinize an arcane cosmic stratagem in which humankind was thunderously coerced away from the truth about pain. Does this imply that before we were given the blinders of ignorance, the truth literally hurt so much that we desperately required anesthetic bliss? Absolutely, yes. Indeed, without fear, guilt, and blame, those three stooges of plump insults du jour, the menacing shadows in our sorrows loomed abundantly too weighty. Weighty, as in pounds? Though allusion, anthropomorphism, aphorism, antithesis, authorial intrusion, analogy, allegory, and an entire alphabet's worth of literary devices swing like vines through the jungle of my writing, I in point of fact unequivocally mean *weighed more*. On the face of it, concepts of astrophysics might seem an odd component of this predominantly philosophical study. Yet I resolve to knit astronomy's bulky orphaned twins, dark matter and dark energy, into sweaters to warm us in the cold of truth's cavernous, yawning emptiness. Through this new, dark lens, we can accordingly discern the objective heaviness we unconsciously conceal through our insults-upon-injuries, ignorant-bliss paradigm. We will untangle how the rose-colored lens of the human mind is prejudiced toward seeing light, conveniently overlooking the cumbersome, scientifically overabundant darkness. Or as that premier salmon swimming against the tide of popular thought, Dr. Carl Jung, once presaged, "There is no coming to consciousness without pain. People will do anything, no matter how absurd, to avoid facing their own soul. One does not become enlightened by imagining figures of light, but by making the Darkness conscious."

And by making the darkness conscious, we get hold of what our species now so spectacularly lacks. That deficiency we hobble along with is of a straightforward, guilt-free, and blame-free elucidation for why the pains of life must pass through us, one and all. And *no*, it's not nature's way of telling us something is wrong. And *no*, it's not God's punishment for original sin. And *no*, it's not given to us as *lessons*. And *no*, it's not there as a contrast so we can know *pleasure*, its opposite sensation. No, no, no, no! In its unqualified embodiment, the pain has virtually nothing to do with us. It predated us. We are merely instruments that the infinite created out of *its need* to heal the raw density of the primordial compression.

Seven and a half billion hoodwinked denizens experience trials we all erroneously attribute to one presumably preventable blameworthy or guilt-worthy circumstance or another. Some say their agony is their *emptiness*, while others cry out that they are *full* of trepidation. Some proclaim that their pain is that they are not loved enough, while others bemoan their own inability to love. Some avow that their distress is their race, gender, religion, or sexual proclivity, while those who throw stones in glass houses are cut to shreds and hoisted on their own petards. Some are convinced their grief is their poverty, while the billionaire asserts his anguish is because his progeny pretends to love him while only lusting for his money. Some are even inexplicably relieved when their doctor furrows his brow and eruditely clumps their suffering into cherished compartments, such as cancer or chronic fatigue or catalepsy or cholecystitis. Some voice their angst as being their inability to score chicks, while the great young actor torments himself because while everyone thinks he should be exultant that he is handsome, rich, famous, sexy, and talented, dark matter and energy are swallowing him whole. (Think Heath Ledger or Phillip Seymour Hoffman.)

When you have waded through the dense swamp of disguised reality that has heretofore kept dark matter and energy utterly buried, you may discern the reservoir of this mysterious cosmic essence lurking just beyond the *no man's land* that separates your soul and your gut. So, raise your hand if anyone has ever scornfully rolled his or her eyes at you as you explicitly described making a crucial decision based on a 'gut feeling.' Next time people condescendingly ooze forth with their analytical arrogance, you'll be prepared with these two bombshells for them. A robust ninety-five percent of the antidepressant neurotransmitter, serotonin, resides not in the brain as we naturally presume but in the enteric nervous system, our gut. Furthermore, one hundred million neurons, slightly more than in the entire spinal column and peripheral nervous system, reside in this enteric gut/mind as well.

Akin to an affluent man handing spare change to a beggar, the hoity-toity human neo-cortex has condescendingly dropped a few coins into the can of the enteric nervous system. Our science has given these one hundred million neurons in the digestive tract the moniker 'the second brain.' How generous! The top-hat-heavy, supposed 'first brain' is an outdated patriarch, blustering on about the need for rationality; all the while suffocating our gut instincts and the serotonin that resides within. Can you say, "Doesn't diminished serotonin lead to depression?" Choke off your gut instincts with heaps of allegedly judicious thoughts, and the serotonin becomes inert, and you, my friend, become moderately depressed or worse.

So let's thank those formerly advantageous thoughts one last time and then send them off to a retirement home. Remember when our thirsty guts told us to go down to that watering hole every morning? And only the saving grace of our commonsensical minds rescued our species? The chest-pounding logic bellows, "*Quad erat demonstrandum*, QED. It is demonstrated, I am the greatest." So let's give that great, thinking mind a righteous retirement party and a gold pen. Let's genuflect and thank it profusely and only then move on into a burgeoning era of fostering our gut instincts and their parasympathetic, plenteous, pain-abating abilities.

Whatever science condescendingly deems to call it, allow me to introduce you to your spanking-new best friend, that one hundred million neurons–strong 'fire in the belly.' Not only is most of your *numero uno* pleasure hormone, serotonin, here in your sacred confidant, but a full fifty percent of another indispensable neurotransmitter, dopamine, resides here as well. While low serotonin, as stated, can lead to depression, other primary disorders such as ADHD, obesity, insulin-resistant diabetes, and higher sensitivity to pain, are all associated with squelched levels of dopamine.

I know we can handle it, but we have work to do. Our guts have been thoroughly frozen out by the societal lock-step consensus of the prefrontal cortex. When our enteric mind organically erupts to grab our attention, our egos gasp, "Uh oh, I think I have anxiety because my gut is stirring up a hornet's nest of buzzing energy." Woefully, these cerebral ego repositories of self-image have already been to court and have been granted full custody of our beings. When the gut cries out and attempts to assert its parental prerogative for even joint custody, the mind tasers us with diagnostic acidity. "Hey, gut," it booms, "if you don't shut the hell up, I'm going to a doctor, and I'm gonna get a righteous diagnosis and drown you in psychotropic medications. Don't think I won't."

Learning then to hear the prototypically understated voice of the id/soul/gut over the mega-phonetically ear-splitting neo-cortex mind is our preliminary assignment. Imagine your psyche getting off its arrogant duff and finally making some good use of itself. Imagine it putting a stethoscope against your gut and listening to the subtle rumblings of those one hundred million soul neurons. Every significant resolution you will render for the remaining days of your corporeal journey will be better made through this stethoscope. Train your mind to be an obedient servant of those rumbles. Remind yourself that as presently constructed, your mind **needs** reminding. Your mentality has become a minefield, all too ready to blow up your enteric soul-scape with its angry, blame-addled, guilty insults. But now, with *stethoscopic* precision, you may begin retraining that mind to hear the thumping pulsation of infinity's ancient drum. While many of you are familiar with the term 'third eye', I beseech you to resolutely develop this gut-listening hearing aid, the 'third ear.'

Fast backward to the commencement of creation. Since every sentient being except humans knows precisely how to react and recover from pain, what was nature or God's deliberate intention behind having us be the only mugs in the world who don't get it? Why are we the ones *adding insult to injury* and thereby suppressing our naturally occurring healing chemicals? Is it just me, or don't we homo sapiens customarily insist that we're cerebrally superior to all the other beasts? Indubitably this is not yet so, but soon I trust. I am convinced that we are destined to one day fully fathom pain's profound status in the universal plan. Our capacity for reasoned thought will in due course cease being the detriment to our lives that it presently is.

As this book will illustrate, all of life was born of two cosmic ingredients. We know them as yin and yang but can just as easily denote them the cosmic light and cosmic darkness, the divine feminine and the divine masculine, the primordial compression that existed before the big bang, and the primordial expansion that has existed ever since, the mother and father, the necessity that was the mother of God's invention, and all that followed the moment it was uttered, "Let there be light." Or, we can simply baptize them pain and healing. However we distinguish them, this narrative will expose that there is a perplexing and paradoxical interplay between the two. Like a train screeching down the tracks with its front wheels askew, sparks flying, and just barely avoiding derailment, all of life's conundrums spring from this wholly veiled holy dysfunction. Furthermore, this alchemic bind has no bright and shiny spontaneous answer as to how it might be overcome and untangled. And since we are hell and heaven bent to believe that everything is perfect in God-land and that all problems arose through human imperfection, the truths exposed within these pages will fly in the face of our reliance on a daddy God cradle. Yet facing this paradox of yin and yang will give us nimble fingers to untangle the degrading *insults upon injuries* knot from which we so urgently require extrication.

When it becomes conceivable to behold the pre-human ultra-contractive sensation of the primordial compression, no longer will we need to concoct insulting motives for why we are experiencing aching bodies, minds, and hearts. Take a big breath. When we can perceive that we were created out of something that is at its epitome, the phenomenon known as *pain,* we may then exalt that the second cosmic ingredient exists solely to *soothe* this infinite tender ache. Instead of believing that all the hurt you ever felt, and are yet to feel, is a deleterious encounter with a regretful fate, how liberating would it be to know that the reverse is entirely correct? The cup is more than half full and is being steadfastly broadened daily by our innate capacity to heal the objective yin material that is at its core, a contractive angst.

With one fell swoop, you are free to throw off the shackles of mortal insult. This is not to say that some of your past discomforts have not been a putrid karmic mess at times. Perhaps some are still oblique and in a foul state of turmoil. Insidiously, this is at the very heart of the *insults on injuries* modus operandi. Our fervent denial of the utilization of our lives as grist for the mill to heal the Primordial Compression, forces us to experience the yin hyper-density in objectionable ways. When we begin to grasp this, we become free to incrementally eliminate victimization, bad karma, accidents, and all the other crap that is presently part of the great insulting subterfuge. When in reaction to all of life's discomfort, we learn to breathe into the contracted thickness of our guts, as a birthing mother brilliantly accomplishes in her sacred labor, we can commence greeting our allotted portion of the primordial compression with dignity. If and when we can even partially initiate this process, we will be flabbergasted by the improvement in our allotments of karma.

CHAPTER 2

The Three Pain/Truth Clichés

And so I don my Don Quixote hat and sword and venture forth to duel the windmills of our self-censoring, blame-spewing, unanimously entrusted bogus dogmata. Yea, with little else to embolden me, I give thanks for my true to life crony, my own Sancho Panza, the *cliche*. Without its platitudinal, hypnotic sweet-talking, I am but another bedraggled dreamer. Without its memorable captivating banality, I am thrashing naked against the thoroughly entrenched human assumption that agony requires unconditional circumvention. I am banging on a metal pot, howling from the mountaintop. I am screaming that despite pain hurting, sometimes throbbing horribly, and sporadically aching so bad there's virtually no way we can bear it, that ushering it into our forbearance with even minimal equanimity, is our triumphant foreordainment. I am inveighing that the cryptic pulse of life is that we were crafted with the sole intent to be remedial magic for every pain we face, in amenity of the cosmic hunger.

For this convoluted Sherlock Holmes mystery then, I enthusiastically offer to you that trio of wily amigos, the *three truth clichés*. Quick, which is bliss, the truth or ignorance? Which hurts, the truth or ignorance? Luckily, though *ignorance is bliss* and *the truth hurts*, at the end of the day, the trifecta of platitudes culminates with *the truth sets us free*. Otherwise, I apparently shouldn't have bothered grinding right up against ignorant bliss with my literary Sisyphus-like endeavor.

Let us imagine a stage far back on the wheel of time. God has sprinkled some of his magic into each soul so that they can use that enchanted substance to remedy a small piece of the primordial angst. Creation has fleetingly offered hope it might flourish, until abject and total failure out of the blue loomed dead ahead on the horizon. And why might catastrophe have approached so in the blink of an eye? Simply this: if ignorance is bliss, the lack of ignorance was what? The antonym for bliss is *misery*. God precisely beheld his experimentation slipping into demise as the burdensome misery of truth relentlessly swallowed the verve in the eyes of his children.

As exhilarating as it momentarily had been for the earliest humans to experience some minimal capacity at alchemizing pure density into amended and lightened *prana*, human memory slowly but persistently propagated into an albatross. In other words, the early humans began to know (remember) what God knew. When homo sapiens were biblically castigated for having eaten of the tree of knowledge of good and evil, that fruit was hardly new but rather had been merely stashed away in the archetypal unconscious. There is a Hebrew term for the confluence of opposites (such as *good and evil*), which is known as a *merism*. A merism pairs these opposites together to connote a larger concept, which signifies 'everything'. So while we say the tree of knowledge of good and evil (in English), in Hebrew, they were implying the tree of knowledge of everything. By remembering, or knowing, *everything* that God knew, humans were starkly reminded of the utter suffocating immensity of the primordial compression from whence they had sprung. The misery of knowing what God knew was that a vast horror had become unobstructed. This dreadfulness was that God's prodigious audition of human life might more than likely fail to heal the immensity. As astronomers to this day solemnly forebode, it is probable that in the end, the universe will contract back into the still-overwhelming gravity of the primordial compression. I have confidence in this not being the ultimate fate, but cosmic triumph is far less than a given.

Furthermore, with a glaring pair of clues peeking out from behind God's trench coat, the Bible spills a few outrageous beans. "And the Lord God said, 'Now that the man has become like one of ***us***, knowing good and evil, he must not be allowed to stretch out his hand and also take from the tree of life and eat, and live forever." Like one of *us*? You mean Daddy's been cohabitating up there in heaven behind our backs? Is the Bible egging us on about a female companion for God? Since we obviously have women and not just men on earth, is it not apparent that we were made in *Gods'* image rather than *God's* image? A series of Bible stories and a Testament later, long after Eve has Eve-ally gotten on with the snake and made Adam ultra-aware of her genitals, Jesus's abject suffering on the cross will entitle him to take from the tree of life, eat, and live forever. Why then had they expressly forbidden Adam from tasting eternal life? If Eve was at fault, branded with fig leaves for making Adam feel diminished by her genital vastness, why deny her boy/toy victim eternity? Is it that Eve's dalliance with the snake had burst Adam into consciousness of good (sexual pleasure) and evil (the primordial compression Eve housed in her genitals)? And, was this already just about too much expansion for his male nervous system to bear? If he had then tasted of eternity and been exposed to the never-ending responsibility to *heal pain,* his tenuous grip on life, on maleness, and on an egoistic self might have been untenable. Instead the Gods introduced the opposite of eternity, *death,* into the equation. Death then would become the nexus of fear and scare the humans into believing that the cessation of life was evil and survival was good. Thus ensnared in this simple black-and-white paradigm, people could unlearn what the Gods knew.

They could disremember the forbidden truth, forgetting that the primordial compression from whence they had arisen was every moment pumping density into them. They could forget God's demand that their assignment was to lighten this eternally dense dark dynamism and forgetting that women's wombs and genitals teemed with a life force that bordered on shocking men into blinding fear. We thus grew to believe that the purpose of our lives revolved around the avoidance of pain and death, the protecting and pleasing of self, and the blustery arrogance of the male psyche. Oh my!

The ultimate commitment of this manuscript is to illustrate how readers will be individually enabled to deduct aspersions from their injuries, yet I would be remiss not to mention nationalistic insults as well. When societies hell-bent on building fortresses around their communal ignorant bliss experience pain, they are wont to make war upon or ethnically cleanse themselves of those they ever-so-conveniently deem as having been responsible for their discomforts. This mass ethnic and religious abusive rhetoric has greased the machinery for the powerful to hypnotize the masses into fighting their wars. With side effects like these, we might become compelled to consult our physician before continuing the ignorantly blissful medicine of our egos. But the paradox of pain versus numbing bliss is vast. Must ignorance continue to rule the day because it temporarily keeps the hounds of painful truth at bay? As my Jewish forebearers might have rhetorically implied: "What's not to like about ignorance? It's blissful!"

As far back as oblivious banality goes, life has always been a game of musical chairs. Everybody meets in the supermarket, and as the hackneyed muzak lulls us ever deeper into zombified triviality, each of us guarantees the other that in answer to the de rigueur query, *"How are you"?* is the equally obligatory rejoinder, *"Fine."* The next day when the music has momentarily stopped in its Circadian-like rhythm, the denouement of the game comes, and one of us must seatlessly lay down in the cold arms of the whirlpool of destiny. Chillingly, one of our cheery friends from the day before has shot himself in the head. It seems that since he found out the week before that his wife was likely having an affair with his best friend, there was a bit of misrepresentation in his breezy "fine" retort at the market. But that's how the game is played. Ignorant bliss requires, nay demands that we play our musical chairs, as if the melody will never stop, and one of us won't have to slip unseated beneath the illusion of pain-averse normality.

And thus, this book is offered in trust that we are close to mature enough to jettison our acquiescence to being forbidden the wisdom of the Gods. A wisdom, I might add, that would allow as to relinquish the need to lie and always claim to our neighbor that everything is hunky-dory. A sagaciousness, that would free us of issues, triggers, Freudian burdens, traumas, and the Gordian knot of believing that the winner of the human race is she or he who outsmarts pain most proficiently.

Pain

Programmed to *conceal* it,
yet when we can *reveal* it
and without insult *feel* it,
spontaneously we'll *heal* it.

Can you envision the master intelligence of a God, nature personified goddess intelligence, or both, conspiring to repay the pain of weightlifters with gain while excluding the rest of us? Having been a bohemian snob in high school, our civil rights marching, folk singing, anti-war crowd beheld ourselves too far above the hoi polloi to participate in organized ruffian athletics. So it is with penitent expressions of regret to the football players and other 'jocks' that we pooh-poohed in those days that I now come cap in hand with a sizable request. As a wannabe philosopher, I'm begging you (down on my knees, flat out pleading with you) to allow me to use your sweat-infused and damn brilliant prosaicism, *no pain no gain*. I mean, no joke here, you can still use it as well. But can you just envisage all the people with physical or psychic hurting and the emancipation they will experience if those four divine words could be realistically utilized outside the gym, track meet, and health club? Maybe I am not yet beseeching you heavy lifters wholeheartedly enough. Let me have another crack at this. Buddha and Christ endeavored fervently but futilely to elucidate the reality you so adroitly accomplished with just a few grunts, newly bulging physiques offering immediate gratification to the burning muscles that had just preceded it. God might have been more stirring when answering Christ's agonizing plea, "Why have you forsaken me?" But let's face it, if Big G had only had time for a four-word reply to His Son, it would have been, yup, *"No pain, no gain."* Whether or not we view the crucifixion from a purely biblical perspective, it was incontrovertibly demonstrated that *tremendous pain begat enormous gain*.

And so, it is computer update time. The prefrontal cortex's ardent determination to harken back to a time when pains were likely to lead directly to demise must finally stand down. I get it, you human brain, you. Back in the day, pain was often a pretty accurate harbinger of death, as it left us vulnerable to a gaggle of gnarly predators. This is no longer true, however. The cavalry has arrived (in the form of grunting weightlifters) just in time to remind us of this profound axiom. Our fear-based neo-cortex causes infinitely more harm than it prevents. It is the time in our human evolution to stop adding insult to our injuries and instead add meaningful, realistic compliments to the wound that conjoins us. What glory if as healers, lovers, and friends, we responded straight-faced to people's heartrending pronouncements about physical or psychic rawness. "I fathom how rotten that pain feels to you at this moment, but thank goodness it will pass, and there will be an actual gain you are accruing through bearing it."

"A literal benefit," their raised eyebrows will colloquially solicit in reply. "Do you mean scientifically actual?" Yes, here goes. We are accustomed to individuals posing what I dub the Freudian question of themselves: "Who am I?" The answer to this inquiry delineates the unique contour of one's singular conscious and personal unconscious apparatus. But more profoundly we could pose the transpersonal query, "What am I?" Now while psychologists favor their patients' "who" ripostes about the self, we philosophers consider we have deeper fish to fry. For us, "What am I?" supplants the "Who am I?" microscope with a telescope. This broader lens of *what we are* leads us into realms of cosmic or theological purpose and meaning of life.

During the Holocaust in WWII, a woefully grandiloquent inquiry was agonizingly posed time and again: "How could a loving God allow all this suffering?" Indeed, if we are to maintain a naive relationship with our Father God, one couldn't help but wonder how Daddy could sanction all the sorrow that humanity endured in that horrific conflagration. But what if at the moment of the big bang, the great plan of God blew the heretofore intractable density of the primordial compression into smaller pieces. Along with many other layers and levels of God's experimentation, he eventually comes up with a paramount invention, the human being. This being embodies the collective soul that contains fragments of the yin primordial compression and an individual soul that is part of God's yang propensity to heal and lighten compressed energy. So as mind-blowingly sad as the Holocaust and much of human history have been (and still is), I am ultimately persuaded that there is unequivocally an end in sight. And not a single drop of the tsunami of this human suffering has been for naught. Am I forgiving or condoning the Holocaust and all the indescribable horrors of history? I know, I know! We sometimes only feel we can keep our heads barely above the flood if we are allowed to at least puff out our chests in horrified indignation about the terrible sufferings of this world. I feel the same way, except these sufferings will only cease when we learn how to alchemize the *one pain* consciously. That's what I'm trying, as best I can, to ease along here, the great catch-22.

It is time to give the neo-cortex its well overdue computer update, to tell the father and mother that we children are ready to accept the mantle of our sacred purpose. Though the journey from living ego-driven lives to living fully in the service of the cosmic necessity may take a breath or two, imagine this choice. You can have a life infused with karma-driven physical and psychic discomforts, and continue to pity yourself that but for a bad break or two, you should not have had to experience those trials. Or you can know that your evolving soul was once part of that which was in a state of eternally painful compression. Talk about a cup half full!

Chapter 3

Chronic Pain Care's Waterloo

During the erstwhile days of Medicine's use of opioids for chronic pain, patients still often withstood a greater portion of their distress than they found pacifying. Then in the later part of the twentieth century, a halcyon shift ensued, and the medical establishment began to consider it tantamount to malpractice to allow patients to undergo significant levels of physical discomfort. In that budding era of "thou shalt not physically suffer," physicians benevolently elevated patient levels of narcotic pain medication until virtually all the agony was gone. In a scrupulously altruistic illustration of "if you've got it, flaunt it," it was deemed cruel to let people agonize when dosages of opiates could be modulated upward until they were significant enough to allay all discomfort exhaustively.

Fast-forwarding to the present, the pendulum has swung radically too far. More Americans currently die from doctor-prescribed narcotic pain meds than from illicit heroin and cocaine overdoses combined. Consequently, a glacial adjustment is underway in the methodology doctors must utilize to interact with their chronic pain patients. If you were to survey medical practitioners as to what single treatment issue most vexes them, I daresay an adamant majority will shake their heads and reply, "chronic pain care." This is an emergent and tragic challenge for countless well-intentioned physicians. The medico-legal associations are in a huge about-face. As if amnesiac about their former culpability, they are currently on the prowl for over-prescribers. The heat is on, and in this cauldron of hushed agony for providers, it is little wonder that they often relate to pain patients as wretched antagonists in a wicked Greek tragedy.

And in spite of the precipitously mounting prescription narcotic deaths, even still the number of pain patients daily morphing into medically induced addicts continues to rise. As extensive studies kept expanding our knowledge of the physical and psychological ill effects of long-term prescription narcotic use, the health care system attempted to swerve and miss the *Titanic* iceberg. Forsooth, as the musicians playing atop deck the sinking ship woefully attest, leaky lifeboats and a frigidly perplexing outlook persist in looming ominously.

As practitioners scramble skittishly to avert becoming the next doc liable for a prescription drug overdose, interactions with patients turn ever more contentious. At facilities across the land, the pain-weary storm from their appointments in an ill-tempered abyss, carping that their doctor has accused them of being drug addicts. Countless others seeking to refill their customary pain med allocation brood that their physician has inferred that their pain levels are being exaggerated. When these sufferers hear that they are to be weaned off their pain- killers whether they like it or not, by God they do not like it. And whereas we humans are hardwired to assess conflict in clear-cut terms of good guys and bad guys, doctors and patients alike are simultaneously blameless and rebuked in this pugilistic tug-of-war for the collateral damage wrought.

Unquestionably, rampant abuse of the opiate medicines presently prescribed for patients exists. Yet, who can say how many addictions might have been circumvented had not a well-meaning bygone physician suggested that increase in dosage? Many docs are self-aware enough to see medicine's culpability in this cruel cause and affect and can't help but be angst-ridden. Furthermore, rather than fulfilling their dream to alleviate suffering, they are currently called upon to take away their patients' presumed panacea. And the resentment, fear, anger, and hatred these patients express toward them, has in turn forced practitioners to don adversarial armor. An artless optimist like Nancy Reagan could blithely profess that "Just say no" had a definite prescriptive potency in its grandmotherly guilelessness. Practitioners, however, weighted by realism, are all too cognizant of the paucity of comforting rhetoric that might be shared with those they are about to wean and temporarily strip of hope. So while the past has been forged in mirthless enigma, and the present unfolds paralyzed in a quagmire of fear, the future perhaps offers us machetes to chop through this jungle of impasse.

While medicine can be forgiven for longing for the good old days when a Jonas Salk could obliterate a calamitous disease with a single swath of brilliance, future resolutions involving pain relief will likely forge ahead far more modestly. So despite the un-magical trudging drudgery that prescription narcotic use presently swallows us in, we can methodically unscramble this. To initiate this evolution via you doctors who work with these patients, you can only make a first impression once. It thus behooves you to embrace that how you come off in the initial moments of your sobering weaning discussion will color the entire interplay to follow. Don't save your most potent compassion merely for those with a new cancer diagnosis. Your narcotic-addicted patients are as genuinely in the throes of terror as anyone with a medically ordained death prognosis. Unless you double majored in mind reading as well as medicine, there is nary an absolute way to verify the severity of your patient's subjective experience of pain. Since agony is as much a product of perception as it is of objective fleshly impediment, one's discomfort is as grievous as one perceives it to be.

As a medical hypnotherapist and doctor of chiropractic, much of my practice naturally revolves around chronic pain management. I treat a number of disgruntled patients who bemoan the ordained impending decrease in their narcotic dosages. Humbly, I offer them the following parable as a way to mitigate the looming fray. For those of you who treat patients about to be weaned off pain meds, please feel free to use it, personalize it as you wish, and by all means, offer it as if it truly occurred.

Recently a weekend adventurer was hiking alone up on Mount Shasta. As he gazed out on the majestic vista to snap a photo, he lost his footing and began plunging toward certain death. Astonishingly, a tree arrested his fall, and he grasped onto the woody savior for dear life. Through the terrifying night and most of the next day, he clung, shivering, to that wooden edifice as his deliverer. Late the second afternoon, rescuers with a rope came along and yelled down that they would pull the frightened nature lover to safety. But the hiker cleaved so desperately to the tree and refused even to consider letting go with one hand to grab the rope. Eventually, a rescuer was lowered down and attempted to wrap the rope around the petrified wayfarer. For the hiker, initially screaming and resisting the rescuer's efforts, the rugged sapling had taken on mythic proportions as his single barrier forestalling death. In the end, thank God, he was raised back to safety and was elated to have been given the opportunity to live appreciatively ever after.

If your patient does not immediately grasp what this homily is hinting at, I would inquire if she were relieved that the rescuer overcame the hiker's initial resistance and was able to save him. Getting an affirmative response is a gateway to getting you and the patient on the same page. Even if they sense where this is going, and their confirmatory reply is a partially begrudging acknowledgment, the desperate hiker/rescuer anecdote reframes the challenge ahead. And you, my compassionate doc, have been designated as what you truly are: *the rescuer*. Concurrently, the patient's warranted resistance has been treated with the dignity it so richly deserves. Of course, the patient is afraid to let go of the tree (the pain medication). Who among us is not addicted on one level or another to something, be it food, coffee, the internet, or a less than thoroughly healthy activity or psychic mind-set that mitigates our suffering?

Yes, you are the liberator, and this is not at all antithetical to your duty to lower the level of the patient's medications. If you can embody the big picture, that there are no bad guys in this grueling tug-of-war, you can alleviate much of the resistance ahead. Keep empathy high and judgment at bay. The more you revere the patient's 'clinging to the tree' in reaction to what you are about to propose, the more he or she will behold you as rescuer and not accuser. Bridge any adversarial distance between you and the patient by openly admitting that once upon a time, doctors (just like yourself) thought it wise to give large doses of narcotics. You might say, "Just as we have always been compelled to adjust medical protocol that proved to do more harm than good, new pearls of wisdom have led us to this moment.

Tongue in cheek, you might ask the patient to spend an hour hanging out at his or her local drug store and say, "Next time you come see me, tell me how many bear, deer, eagles, or wolves stop there to pick up pain meds. In other words, do you believe that animals do not experience pain? Or is it that they just have a better way of dealing with it? I always thought that humans were the smartest animals, but all these other critters have a much healthier way to deal with agonizing physical impediments. They lay down, rest, and allow their naturally endowed endorphins and immune systems to heal them. Unlike us, they do not add insult to injury by flooding their bodies with endorphin-suppressing fear neurotransmitters in response to pain. Nature did not treat our four-legged friends to an exclusive design denied the two-legged. Your body and mind's aptitude to generate relief and restoration is a great miracle. And though life-saving medicines and other twenty-first-century medical breakthroughs are a glorious addition to nature's work, God certainly was not showing cruelty all those thousands of years before pharmacies were invented. No, we were designed as well as He did all the beasts of the field. Who the heck do you think does a better job: life itself making perfect morphine (endorphins) in your body, or a factory pumping out generic morphine pills for those not yet privy to the gifts we share in common with animals?"

I can imagine many of you docs shaking your heads, snickering that not only could you never see yourself pulling off the above scenario, but that even if executed adroitly, patients are not so easily cajoled into compliance. Look, I agree. Many patients will be only slightly more amenable to change after my suggested dog and pony show above. But if even a third of these patients are genuinely moved by your effort to address their concerns humanely, you will sleep soundly in the cognizance of your newly expanding repertoire.

A further bonne bouche on the subject of suffering is that most of our mommies and daddies, overtly or covertly, implied that if we followed their parental instructions to a 'T', they would successfully shield us from discomfort. When Ma and Pa Kettle's impossible promise proved to be a pipedream, a resentful archetype toward parental figures built up in the human collective unconscious, one disgruntled child at a time. So the patient takes one look at you and feels, "Here comes another mommy or daddy wiener (wean-er), demanding me to roll over and play dead as they fail to protect me from my pain." Sorry, Doc, I know you wrestle with overt and covert negative transference consistently aimed at you. So face it right on. Bring this up to your patients, how their parents with good intentions gave their children the absolute wrong message about pain.

And then there is a crusade in consciousness that you might chew over before you ask your patients to alter their pain-averse fear-based attitudes. An old maxim about pain was that it was nature's way of telling us that something is wrong. And because we practitioners consider it incumbent to solve what is wrong, we mistakenly overmedicated and became accessories to the crime we are now agonizingly unraveling. A fresher aphorism about physical suffering offers us a vibrant new grasp of nature's ubiquitous and unkind sensation: "No pain, no gain." Could someone ever climb Mount Everest without this truth infusing every cell of his or her body, every neuron in his or her brain, and every instinct in his or her gut and soul? Could a long-distance runner ever complete a marathon, gutting through the wall of agony until he or she reached the hallowed runner's high? I like to ask my patients, "Do you think God is some jock-lover, where he would only give gain to athletes for their pain and not the rest of us?"

And what of mothers and their passionate willingness to go through contractions and labor pains to continue the propagation of humanity? Is the gain for the pain here not evident enough? A few generations ago, almost every mother gave birth in a hospital, getting shot up with enough painkillers to drop a horse. Now, whether with home births, birthing centers, or more conscious hospital births, the trend is toward delivery without numbing amendments. Why would women evolve away from pain suppression toward the innate capacity of their bodies to reward them for the pluck and valor of their anointed gravid enterprise? Because, as a species, we are inexorably being led toward awakening. Agony is an arduous path to traverse but a highly sanctified one nonetheless. Indeed, there are two immeasurably different ways to deal with immediate discomfort. We can numb it, or we can rise through it and exalt the human pathos. The profound gain conceived through the transformation of raw energy into healed substance could not be farther away from the lifeless ennui of benumbed stasis.

CHAPTER 4

Relentless Physical Agony

Some of you physically agonize without medication, a rock and a hard place constricting around you like a boa, growing ever more scornful of your wedged predicament. Or you take these drugs but feel resolute in reducing usage, finding insufferable the way they make you feel so 'out of it.' Most likely, however, you are neither of the above but rather are being strong-armed to wean off your current opiate dosage. You experience yourself being thrown from your lifeboat and scorned for your resistance to drown in an ocean of agony and apprehension. And I get that you may instantly abhor me for reminding you of this, but your doctor is weaning you because those meds are downright awful for you.

Of course, you are rightly unsettled, but allow me to soothe you ever so slightly. For countless thousands of years, our species existed before pharmaceutical companies or drug runners plied their wares. This indisputably corroborates that the body was created with a charming gift to alleviate agony. And I don't want to be flip, but to access this blessing, we merely have to re-evoke its memory. Although this most likely will not be unerringly easy, it is nonetheless abundantly simple. Subtracting insult from your injury will clear negative mind/body neurotransmitter mechanisms and thus allow you to pass through moments of suffering as innately as does a whale, a lion, or an eagle. Before we discuss the steps involved with unblocking this inherent function, we will elucidate a bit about endorphins, the natural pain-killing substance your body has manufactured since the commencement of time.

In the 1970s, researchers studying how the brain is affected by heroin and morphine inadvertently found that these drugs interact with specialized receptor cells in neurons in the brain and spinal cord. As narcotics enter these *opioid receptors*, they effectively hinder the neuron's transmission of pain signals, which then dramatically lightens one's physical distress. But why, wondered the experts studying this phenomenon, would these specialized receptors have unmistakably existed, even before morphine and heroin were ever a twinkle in a drug pusher's or pharmacist's eye? The unambiguous answer was that opioid receptors have always existed in their predestined interplay with an opiate-like substance produced naturally in the body. Endorphins, this chemical bridge over troubled water, is your own private and perfectly self-manufactured narcotic.

Shorthand for 'endogenous morphine,' this elixir is manufactured in the body in immediate response to pain. It originates in the pituitary gland, the spinal cord and throughout the brain and nervous system. It not only blocks pain, but is also responsible for intense sensations of pleasure. The majority of emotions and memories are processed by the brain's limbic system, which includes the hypothalamus, the region that handles a range of functions from breathing and sexual satisfaction, to hunger and emotional response. When endorphins reach the opioid receptors of the highly emotional limbic system, you experience pleasure as well as a cessation of physical discomfort. Anyone who has ever taken an opioid for either pain relief or as a weekend intoxicant will affirm that both reactions are common co-entangled components of the package. Consequently, the addictive potential of externally administered opiates is off the charts.

As the command and control center of your endocrine system, the hypothalamus decides when you need a high dose of endorphins. With pain's onset, it initiates a chain of messages by prompting the pituitary gland to release chemicals that trumpet endorphin-containing neurons to hear the call. Though it might sound too good to be true, when left unobstructed, those happy hormones are thoroughly inexorable.

As to the evolutionary metamorphosis that doomed this slick hypothalamic/endorphin mojo and begat our present dysfunctional relationship to pain, our species' relative physical weakness was again our Achilles' heel. At a moment of Darwinian crossroads, humans were doing quite poorly in the reality show called *Survival of the Fittest*. It had become imminent to convert fear into a far louder voice screaming in our heads than any need for pain cessation. When a human was about to succumb to real danger, it was behooving to forgo the intoxicating pleasantries of endorphins. It was more befitting to immediately release the fight, fright, or flight neurotransmitters and leave pain relief for later. Thus, if a burly, old wooly mammoth was chasing me in the wild, and while running away I fell and broke my leg, survival dictated that fear should trump pain. If my body had released endorphins at that moment, I would have been grooving on the natural narcotic healing high, and the furry one would have quickly caught and quite insouciantly dined on me. Instead, with adrenaline and cortisol pumping me up into a frothing FFF survival mode, it was more in the offing that I fleetly claw my way back home in a frenzy and live to paint my harrowing tale on the walls of the cave. Back in the shelter of my grotto, my swirling, whirling innards would fathom how it was finally safe to release the endorphins for pain relief, healing, sleep, and emotional rebalancing.

And so it went for countless eons. In an otherwise

unforgiving crisis-infused milieu of earthly existence, a balanced evolutionary, biochemical interplay of neurotransmitters took hold as an essential blueprint for the flourishing of humanity. As this particularized retail survival gradually became less of an urgent worry, a second, more insidious wholesale impediment to automatic endorphin response began to take hold. This brutally realistic species-wide tribal exclusion fear essentially went like this: "Oh crap, this broken leg is likely to incapacitate me for so long that the tribe might get sick of feeding me and become compelled to expel me to increase survival benefits for the rest of its members." With this convincing anxiety coursing through my mind and body, fear once again began trumping pain relief and healing. Whether the feelings of impending doom were conscious or unconscious, those trepidations that the tribe could abandon an incapacitated member, once again involuntarily increased adrenaline and cortisol at the automatic expense and suppression of endorphins. So instead of the perfect neurotransmitter balance that had just so recently guaranteed humans such a lofty position on the evolutionary ladder, one's fear of the tribal repercussions of their pains established an archetypal vicious cycle that is to this day cursing our species. This reflexive, subconscious abandonment fear attached to physical pain is a deep well from which self-inflicted insults are to this day abundantly heaped upon our injuries.

And as if this were not enough of an impediment, there's more! Completing the perfect dystopian storm, there is yet a final component in the trifecta of stimuli causing fear neurotransmitters to trump endorphins. Hurtful childhood experiences carve a neural riverbed in our unconsciousness into which insults are involuntarily bred to add themselves to injury. A parent may have reacted to our physical pain with an overt, "Stupid, I told you not to touch the stove" or a covert resentment of us because he or she momentarily felt helpless to solve our pain. Furthermore, an entire array of primal, early childhood realities includes the fact that infancy left us 100 percent at the mercy of every single other person in our orbit of early life. We could not talk or walk or feed ourselves or change ourselves or explain our fears or pains or needs or desires. Instead, all of our earliest feelings consisted of dependence upon those who did everything better than us; and who, depending on their moods, might occasionally fail to take perfect care of us. And rather than learning to embrace that our caregivers' attitudes were nothing we could control or predict, our best bet in those earliest moments was to assume that our behavior was the primary influence of whether care was to be forthcoming or not. So when physiologic and emotional trials flooded our small beings, we trumped endorphin release yet again with fear. Would we be worthy enough to get our needs met, or would some unfathomable shortcoming of ours push our caregivers away? How could we, how would we ever know? The fear chemicals raged … what could we do? Not only were all of these tumultuous sensations of infancy stored away subconsciously, but they were also encoded with horrific emotionally laden thought images. In the present, when pains occur, the memory spits up an entire short story's worth of these haunted house "gotchas." Oh, what crawling creatures of the mind emerge from this canister in the guise of entirely believable fear skyscrapers!

Then, once the neurotransmitters of fear are coursing through our bodies, the mind reacts to them by assuming that what they are signaling is a *real*, and not just a perceived, threat. Fear, as thought and emotion, leads to the release of fear neurotransmitters, which re-signal the brain that there is something dire going on, and so on and so forth. This vicious cycle not only festers like a virulent, self-propelling motion, but the poor orphaned physical agonies that only needed a few good endorphins, are left shivering out in the cold.

Ah, but there is an abundant opportunity for us to identify the progression of cascading thoughts, feelings, and chemical responses that constitute the malicious cycle. Auspiciously, like any perpetual-motion construct, subtract one insult from the injury, and the negative albatross can crumble like a house of cards. Subtracting insult from injury is potent because once we successfully remove the impediment, the body knows precisely what to do. We have nary a need to teach the body how to relieve our pain! Endorphins are waiting like caged animals, ready at a moment's notice for us to subtract the outdated, unreasonable reasons we have given the body to trump pain with fear.

Because you now know that fear is a preprogrammed, obsolete, no longer indispensable reaction to pain, you are being unconstrained from the primitive reactivity. Ninety-nine percent of the time, no animal is chasing you, no one is about to eat you, and none of your tribe is about to banish you. Ninety-nine percent of the time, you are not enfeebled as if you were still an infant, with some parental figure who was possibly going to fall short of caring for your pain. Ninety-nine percent of the time, your endorphins are raring to go in their genetic impetus to relieve your suffering. Our minds are like computers, ready for an earnest reprogramming. And in ninety-nine percent of situations requiring change, that which we are changing from was scarcely irrational but rather once had mitigating motives for existing. We are not chumps who have sloppily chosen an erroneous path that we must now disavow. We are creations of the Infinite, traversing a span that once upon a time, there was no other choice but to tread upon. So the fear about how tough it will be to wean to a lower dose of medication is but a viaduct from which you are about to dismount finally. Your antennae are percolating, and you are at the very least entertaining this arresting new field of healing we know as mind/body medicine. You are not only poised on the ledge of learning a great new way to deal with your pain, but you are also disembarking from the human fear impulse on the abundant new side of infinite grace.

So although you have grown accustomed to feelings of

abandonment, fear, martyrdom, victimhood, and hypervulnerability all bleeding into your present-day thought process, a massive transformation lies before you. When our egos pout that our discomfort is an evil harbinger of trouble ahead, we are programmed to believe its 'the sky is falling' admonitions. Ah, but the sky is resolutely set in the firmaments, and your body is raring to go in its mission to relieve you and end your pain. When flowing water has been temporarily held back by a log in the river, we do not have to reteach the water how to flow. We just move the log. Water knows how to flow. The body knows perfectly well how to have endorphins flow and alleviate pain. This frankly is a slam-dunk! (Forgive me my boy-boy metaphors)

Though an ego is exceedingly captivated by itself in its assumption that it, and it alone, constitutes what we call the self, at best we should ascribe it the title of chief butler or maid. In this epic epoch where ninety-nine percent of the time we need no patriarchal hyper-logical voice bullying us from within, the ego's job should merely consist of ministering to your connection to the universal plan. Every day, billions of average humans have a semblance of the following confab with themselves. "*I* better control *my* feelings, or *I* will *do* something that makes *me* guilty or regretful." This outward discrepancy about who is the ultimate *I* or *me* is illustrative of Freud's resplendent edification of the multicolored aspects of a self. The ego in its relationship to the id, the actions of that id, and the consequences of that action as perceived by the super-ego are all quite transparent. If I (ego) do not control my anger (id) I might yell at my boss (action id), get fired, and then certify myself an idiot for letting my feelings run amok (superego). And since it is thus as barefaced as pie that normal people have this handful of assorted voices in their head, you need not feel like a nut (Almond Joy) to use a nobler voice to correct an old erroneous one. When your ego reacts to your pains in its programmed negativity, you can flex new gut-inspired mental muscles to modify the ego-inspired static.

Your phobic blue funk has just responded to an agony by blaring out that this proves you do not have enough pain medication, and that you can't live and function with so much discomfort. But I'll tell you the only thing it proves: it shows that *you are alive*. What proves something is patently wrong is *being incapable of* experiencing pain. There are two diseases called congenital analgesia and congenital anhidrosis, both of which completely inhibit any sensations of pain.

So when pre-programed faintheartedness screams that the pain you are having is a frightening and dreadful occurrence, another voice inside you may henceforth answer with maturity and clear-headedness:

Yes, this hurts a ton, and I am sure looking forward to it stopping. Thank God my body makes endorphins. As soon as I calm down and take some slow, full-bodied breaths, those astounding endorphins will get underway to ease my pain. I frankly hate this hurting, but there is nothing to fear. The worst is nigh o'er, and the endorphins itching to jump into action. Pain is rough, but what a boundless relief knowing my body is built to ease this discomfort.

In my chiropractic practice, I have numerous patients in their seventies, eighties, and even nineties who come to me with longstanding chronic pain. And with extremely gentle non-manipulative treatments, their suffering often significantly diminishes or disappears. And this principally occurs because I sense and contact the impetus in their bodies that is rarin' to hum into endorphin release. My treatments are specifically intended to activate it, but truly without any complicated technique. The patients' degenerative disc disease and severe arthritis certainly aren't going away. But their pain often is! If your chronic pain is not abating, most likely your nervous system got stuck in the cruel cycle of fear trumping pain relief.

What's more, if you are Christian, try this on for size. For being God's favorite child, Jesus did not get an all-expenses-paid vacation to some Mediterranean island. God's beloved Son was asked not just to die (which could have been accomplished in about a minute), but to withstand an inconceivable depth of pain. God needed this of His Son, imploring Jesus to *experience* all of His agonies. He needed Jesus to become the blueprint—needed him to teach the rest of us to stop resenting our portion of the primordial compression he had created us to embody and make well. Through Jesus's triumph, the biggest "no pain, no gain" in history transpired. In Jesus's accomplishment, your path has been forged. (And by the way, I am not even remotely a Christian but a mishmash of many philosophies.) Like Jesus, you can temporarily lose faith and wonder if God has forsaken you and then discover in the end that He hasn't. Like Christ's redemptive trials, your agonies can become the sacred substance of infinite transformation. When you survive them without holding them in resentment, you fulfill the very reason for your creation. It is no coincidence that the word *heavy* and the word *heaven* are so alike. When we accept God's universal need for us to incrementally lighten the massive energy we experience as pain, we help create rehabilitated heaviness (a.k.a., heaven).

CHAPTER 5

The Question of Pain, Answered

Here's an irony plodding like an elephant through our collective experience. We know it is a primary responsibility of an ego to leave no stone unturned in nourishing every famished question with the red meat of a self-assured, buoyant answer. You name a query, and if your mind can't solve its mini-mystery, your internet will. And heaven forbid if it can't electronically do the deed, you'll hire a guru, and he will mega-confidently make sure every lonesome question doesn't stay unhitched long. Hell, sometimes it isn't even the crux of the problem to find the definitive spot-on answer; you can just parrot whatever the majority of others are saying. The point is, we are hip post-modern humans, and at the very least, we are genetically determined and inclined to act as if unanswered questions are tantamount to imbecility. Worse, unrequited queries are akin to being nonhuman (like those stupid animals that couldn't give a shit).

The enormous irony is that while most questions grow obese, fast-food answers compulsively crammed down their throats, one itty-bitty wide-eyed query whimpers in the corner, malnourished to the max. Whether we are Christians or not, why do we accept the truth or myth that God ordered his *favorite* human to undergo such vast agony on the cross? Why did the cherished child have to suffer so exquisitely for God? If he merely had to die for our sins, I've said it before, dying only takes about a minute. But suffering on the cross for hour upon hour? And if you don't believe the crucifixion even happened, why do you guess that billions of other humans do nonchalantly accept that God had his favorite child writhe endlessly in abject torture? And last, if Christ was indeed following God's directive, pleasing his Father through surrender to such agony, why do the rest of us regard ninety-nine percent of our pains as if they are to be met with petulant blame or guilt? This is the absurdity! God's favorite undergoes huge pain, and the rest of us abrasively harrumph, "God damn it" when some kid accidentally steps on our foot in front of the church.

One of my daughters once pointed out to me that the word *question,* when serendipitously broken down into its two component syllables, forms a 'quest ion.' For those of us who remember some high-school chemistry, any ion worth its salt is premeditated to attract its complementary ion. Two hydrogen ions seek out a sexy oxygen ion for a chemical ménage-a-trois, and voila, we are enhanced by water. A worthy quest ion thus should be hanging out at the coolest chemistry café flirting, until it can attract a suitable answer ion. And yet assuming it is too shy, I offer to the question of how we can solve our pain by cultivating the activation of endorphins, the ANSWER: Autonomic Nervous System's Wisdom: Endorphin Release. This autonomic nervous system state of natural pain relief can be attained through hypnosis, meditation, prayer, exercise, conscious breathing, tapping, and a laundry list of other modalities. The autonomic (automatic) nervous system is the spontaneous, involuntary part of our nerve pathways that when unimpeded, automatically keeps our body regulated and functioning. The autonomic nervous system's wisdom spontaneously includes endorphins and their perfect reaction to pain. The A.N.S.W.E.R. was once the body's inherent response to pain and with some effort, will be that again, but for now … Yes, blokes and lasses, for now, we've got ourselves a wee bit of work to do.

As counter-intuitive as this may seem, ninety-nine percent of the time we need not be figuring out specifically *why* we have every individual pain. It just does not matter. If in your meditation or prayer you find a few lucid moments of *know*ing that the body's wisdom will ease the pain, that tiny glimpse of transcendence reignites the extinguished flame of healing. Remember, if God takes away the pain of weightlifters and long-distance runners and gives them gain, c'mon be real; of course, he's about to take yours away as well. Take a soft, deep breath. The body is impetuous, dying to flaunt its stuff. Say out loud or under your breath:

> I hate this pain and can't wait until the endorphins kick in. I hate it I hate it I hate it! *But* there is nary a need for worry. I hate it, *but* there's no life-and-death reason for me to fear it or learn some profound lesson from this pain. I hate it, it hurts … I can't take much more, *but* I won't have to. Any minute I will relax into the crest of the wave, the easing of the pain.

And to that end, I present:

Autonomic Nervous System Wisdom: Endorphin Release

The A.N.S.W.E.R.

It might make sense to read through the set of instructions once, and then come back and go step-by-step through the experience. If you desire and you have a loved one with whom you feel comfortable going into swirling waters, invite her to be present. She *need not do or say anything*, just simply be a grounding love holding your hand. If you feel more contented doing this kind of exercise alone, great. And if you are anything like me, and hate techniques that demand absolute faithfulness to meticulous steps and precise execution of tasks, you're in luck. No matter how you do the ANSWER, you're going to be heading down the river of healing in the right direction. I have just sketched a pathway for you; color it in any way you wish. And though this set of exercises is initially intended to ease physical suffering, it is readily adapted as well for emotional angst.

THE ANSWER

1. Get ready to descend into The Autonomic Nervous System's Wisdom: Endorphin Release......the ANSWER. Without an intoxicant, painkiller, guru, or a healer present, you are about to move the needle in the right direction. I absolutely guarantee that your time spent here will reap some well-earned experience. Spend a few minutes tuning into your physical and/or emotional pain. Get close to it, and observe the details of experience:

a. Feel the sensations. Where in your body are they?
b. What images and emotions accompany the agony?
c. Is this thing we call pain cold or burning like hot coal?
d. Is there a color? Is it dark or light?
e. Does it have a voice, and what does it say?

While we humans are biased toward an aversion-centered relationship with our pains, the above exercise and those to follow are designed to cajole our myriad pain antiphons out of the embattled monolithic sarcophagus in which we have encased them. You might find that coupled with your aversion-centered relationship to pain, there can often be a seemingly opposite unconscious clinging to our pain and the multiverse of victimhood it affords us. Without judgment, just notice to what degree this exists inside you and what it perhaps gets you.

2. Mentally tally or write down the insults your brain is adding to your pain. Any resistance you encounter during this process is because, as repulsive as your insults are for you, they have a mind of their own and believe they are staunch soldiers employed for your protection. Any of you remember Hal the Computer clinging to existence in *2001: A Space Odyssey*?
3. See the common theme in the various insults. Reduce it to a phrase, such as need, fear of judgment, resentment, loss, hurt, anger, shame, abandonment, betrayal, or fear of death.
4. Feel that reduced aspect of consciousness that has taken up residence in you. Merge with it entirely, and become so identified with it that you *are* it. Breathe profoundly.
5. Now, shift away from identification with the pain, and establish the sentience that you are *not* your experience. Back away from the sensations, and observe them from a distance.

   Remember: you can have a cold, but no one calls you "cold" as a nickname. You can have pain, but *you are not pain*. You are falling into an original place inside where capacity to behold your pain in a vastly upgraded way is going to turn your *upside-down* world upside-down, so it is finally right side up!

6. Take several moments to settle into who you are that is greater than, *though lovingly includes*, your suffering. Herein lies the capacity to say yes to all the dualistic

experiences of pain and pleasure. Herein lies the capacity for unconditional love of your experience, for *all* that is occurring through you.

7. Thank the ego/butler part of your brain for its faithful service in once-upon-a-time presenting dire possibilities and their emotional add-ons to your pain. They truly once were irreplaceable. The mess we now arise away from, did not have a stupid etiology.
8. Whatever is transpiring let it happen entirely, until the dislodging energy runs its course.

   You are activating an innovative part of yourself (id/big love/Christ consciousness) that stands with the capacity to thank your ego that you once believed was your *whole* self.

9. Scream out loud or imagine screaming at the top of your lungs, "This is unbelievable that I am about to get pain relief from morphine that *my body* is making."
10. Visualize the freedom, time, and possibilities for new experiences you will have when that free morphine starts doing its thing. And by the way, iota for iota, endorphins are thirty-five times as strong as the manufactured stuff.
11. Check if there is a part of you that is afraid of new possibilities. Is there an aspect that contracts around these invitations to expand? If you become free from pain, *then what*? Dive into the mystery, and make none of what you find wrong. You carried this burden a long way. You've done the pain time; it's gain time now! You crossed the pain bridge. You climbed your personal Mount Everest. This is not airy-fairy-ville. This is Nature's impeccable handiwork.
12. Visualize a loving adult who might have said to you as a child, "Let me kiss your boo-boo and take away your pain." Welcome that kiss now. Touch the spot of

pain with your own hand, lips, or heart. Fully receive this healing gift. Next, call to heart your offspring, or someone else you love, and imagine *your* kiss easing *their* anguish. Pay it forward. Invite this to have evolutionary impact through the greater field of life in which you live. And, remember, "First there was the word." Every time I ask you to visualize, or suggest that you say something, the mind's words and pictures are the *exact* way it communicates to your body. And when you add prayer, you're connecting mind, body, and heart/soul to an infinite wisdom, or trusting that words do reach God's ears. For those of you familiar with physicist Bruce Lipton, his seminal work with epigenetics establishes that cells have periscopes that rise from the cell membrane to listen and perceive what messages the mind is using to inform the body.

If you know the technique called *tapping*, you can either do it through the above steps or begin now. *Tapping* essentially tells the body that this is far more than just a mental attempt to change our thinking. This exercise exists to activate our body in its blessed capacity to relieve pain. If you aren't familiar with *tapping*, either learn it online, or frankly, you're also *completely* fine without it

13. The next exercise is called *Two Rivers Running*. The first and most prevalent waterway is the collectively agreed upon river of time that flows from the past into the present and toward the future. It can also be viewed as history, time relentlessly marching on in an often catastrophic mélange of disturbing cause and effect. It is the conventional version of our collective assumption that we behave mostly in reaction to our subconscious

issues. Trauma from the past affects my disposition in the present, which then causes me to treat life a certain way that ripples forward in a contorted attempt to squeeze compliance out of the future. I have nicknamed this convoluted flow of time *the River of Shit* (after a 1960s song by the irreverent band The Fugs).

But alas, there is a second, albeit much smaller, tributary of time as well. This tempo of moving moments is neither motivated nor maneuvered as a byproduct of past trauma or avoidance of future hurt. I call this second waterway *the Trickling Stream of Grace*. Instead of being driven forward in response to the past, it is magnetized toward us (and we toward it). It exists in the future, planted there by a vision, as a grand plan of the infinite consciousness. As the big bang exploded forth, it contained not only the vast energetic power to rupture the primordial compression but also a prescriptive vision as to how and when the culmination of the infinite plan might be realized. Sitting, then, at the end of the Trickling Stream of Grace, like a vibratory finish line to the human race, the blueprint for heaven on earth awaits our arrival. Like a holographic template lying at the end of human history, it broadcasts that one day we humans will have ultimately finished alchemizing the agony of the primordial compression.

And thus, we are free to behold the cosmic purpose behind all our hardships and the astronomic necessity of the big bang that separated us into these individual containers of anguish being alchemized into grace. Through the one eternal memory lying underneath all our human artifice, we are drawn toward this perfect vision. We are predestined to be transformed from victims of our pains into cosmic cylinders using the portion of the primordial compression stored in our soul as fuel to propel us toward the exalted end of universal suffering. And so the exercise proceeds as follows.

As you lay down and experience your angst, picture yourself tumbling down the River of Shit, in the direction of your head toward your feet. All the stories, fears, resentments, and martyrdom, the fort you have built to protect yourself and the hardness in your heart you use to deflect perceived injustices being rained down upon you, are aspects of this human river. It was not you who invented this waterway. Over to the right of this River of Shit flows the eternal Trickling Stream of Grace. Though it exists outside your ego, it is transpiring concurrently with your personalized Greek tragedy. It is using your survival of every single pain you experience to propel the universe toward its appointed mission of transcendent homeostasis. Just ahead there is a canal. It is connected from the River of Shit, perpendicular over to the parallel running Trickling Stream of Grace. Christ and Buddha and a score more saints, mystics, geniuses, and heroes have carved this canal with the resolve of their visionary souls. Mother Theresa, Gandhi, Martin Luther King, Desmond Tutu, Nelson Mandela, and others have widened the channel with the backbone of their convictions. And here you are, one of the very first humans with the faith and capacity to consciously will yourself into this canal. That's right, the above-mentioned champions carved the canal by holding faith with soul imperatives that had annexed and supplanted their human comforts. But your audacious willingness to presently lie at the entrance to this byway, exiting the River of Shit and its misguided credence as *real life,* inaugurates new human hope in consecrating the hallowed efforts of the saints and visionaries who preceded you.

Yes, you are in the canal now, and you never need again accept your ego's old, tired tales about the "poor you" who was victim to circumstance and human misconduct. You are in a birth canal, midwifing yourself toward the Trickling Stream of Grace. You may experience a sense of emptiness here as the ego voids itself of its "full of shit" melodramas. And now you are at the far end of the canal, where the Trickling Stream of Grace is sweeping by. As a caterpillar need expend no earth-shattering effort to trans-morph itself into a butterfly, the trillions of cells that comprise your body and the one hundred million enteric neurons that download your gut instinct and soul communication are already primed for transformation. Like a scuba diver entering the ocean, fall backward into the Trickling Stream of Grace. As it takes you into its fierce and tender knowing, it may feel gentle, but is just as likely to feel like a persuasive current is hurtling you toward the final holograph of God's great vision. By entering this non-egoistic force that runs parallel to the River of Shit, you are embarking upon your Swadharma. Without going too deep into this concept, swadharma is your very personal highest authentic living out of your kismet, destiny, or karma. So while this state of being still revolves around this entity known as YOU, it is not being coerced by your ego's fears, narcissistic manipulations, or fantasies. Swadharma can still feel daunting, but it is your loftiest calling. You're gonna like it.

14. There is a Buddhist exercise known as *tonglen,* that is practiced somewhat as follows: A meditator pictures

herself pulling the tribulations of another into her own being. Once this troubled energy is inside her, her heart's willingness to embrace rather than avert herself from struggle lights a mystical pilot light. This flame uses the dense primordial compression she has pulled from the other as fuel for a fire, which begets a passionate glow. The travail has been transformed into this glowing energy, which she then sends back to the former sufferer in a glorious new form. Occasionally tonglen is practiced as one meditates on embracing one's own formerly shunned layers of hurt. Again, as the heart sheds its protective layer of aversion toward inner pain, it comports itself as a cosmic combustion engine. It breaks down the actual energetic composition of a pain sensation and re-mixes the ingredients into glowing embers of grace. This is precisely the micro version of the macro phenomenon transpiring in the Trickling Stream of Grace.

15. Next, we will employ a principle of physics called the law of quantum possibility. Roughly stated it means this: Before a moment occurs in the present, the energy and matter that must coalesce to create that instant of observable human time exists (in a type of pre-moment) in many possible forms. If we can shake the habitual prefabricated logic we deem to be reality, quantum possibility makes a ton of sense. Above all, it is sympathetic to God's colossal task of creating trillions of possible variable realities for each of us in every moment. And so, despite being the wizard that He is, it makes sense that God needs to do a little prep work before he unfolds each new moment to his 7.5 billion protégées. Based on your recurring knee-jerk reactions to most situations, God has a pretty precise inkling as to how your subsequent moment will look. He prepares the atomic ingredients to craft your specific

moment and can't be caught with his pants down. He needs to be ready first for the highly probable moments that most likely will transpire. Then, in a progressively diminishing cascading continuum, He also gears up for less likely but minimally possible scenarios as well.

The law of inertia in physics states that an object at rest will remain at rest unless acted on by an unbalanced force. An object in motion continues in motion with the same speed and direction unless acted upon by an unbalanced force. This means that there is a natural tendency of life to keep on doing what it's been previously doing. Everything by nature resists changes in their state of motion. And so goes our interaction with the quantum probabilities/possibilities that are presented to us. Unless we apply the unbalanced force of steadfastly choosing a fearless new path, the most probable quantum moment that will transpire is our River of Shit–inspired fort.

Abetting this inertia-laden predisposition to choose comfort over change are two deeply embedded human propensities. First, a person's Darwinian survival chances were phenomenally increased through repeatedly reacting in familiar ways to everyday scenarios. Second, as an infant is faced with the daunting task of learning every single skill that will be depended upon for survival, the quickest path between helplessness and proficiency is the well-trodden repetitive riverbed of absolute conformity to what the child sees everyone else doing. And hence we tend to travel the beaten path to repetitive and bland inertia. Each time we repeat inertia-based, repetitively compulsive, non-evolving reactions to what life offers us, the neural river carves the riverbed ever deeper. Then when God, as the essence of quantum physics, prepares the alchemic probabilities/possibilities for forthcoming moments, he grows accustomed to the fact that you rarely deviate from fort-like probability number one. God will thus invest less cosmic zeal in the hope of you changing than in another who lives life more fearlessly. When we hear that God helps those who help themselves, this no-brainer is because, despite our childlike Daddy obsession about his purportedly unlimited power, he is a busy (and dare I say, limited), Dude. Thus, each time we break the mold and do not acquiesce to the less-evolved known, He is alerted to spend his effort to help strengthen the magnetic inevitability of fresh pathways offering us new landscapes. God made us for a purpose that we are only scratching the surface of approaching. When we open to serve that purpose in a fuller way, God, of course, helps us to help Himself.

16. Continuing on the last theme, the quick quantum quality opportunity (or 3QO) will begin with a visualization of a moat that runs horizontally across your inner eye-scape with your eyes closed. In this moat is the cosmic soup of God's ingredients that await their duty to frame every moment of your life. On the bottom of the trench are a series of drains through which the soup can descend into your life as moments of karmic becoming. On the left-most corner of the moat is the drain for the most probable reaction you will have to any given situation. On the far right is the drain for the least likely, most courageous possibility. As you concentrate on a pain you are presently experiencing, have recently experienced, or dread you are about to experience, imagine your standard default drain on the far left. This drainpipe most likely includes your fears, resentments, and self-loathing surrounding your given hurting. Feel yourself being pulled toward this predictable place on the left. And

now your quantum (3QO) choice to change begins. All that cosmic soup is programmed to acquiesce and pour your precious humanity down its familiar unenthusiastic drain. Yet deep inside your soul is the salmon swimming up-stream toward the right against the river of that greatest probability. And like the salmon, there is more than just a sensation of struggle as you move against the tide. You were built to defy mundane inertia. There are activations and even some elation. With each full-bodied breath, you feel your movement strengthening in your rightward journey. This is yet another journey on the canal away from the River of Shit and toward the Trickling Stream of Grace. Fall once again into the stream, all the way to the right. You are more than a human right now. You are what the Infinite created in its hope to bring forth its envisioned universe.

Even as the above transpires on an extremely subtle plane and your physical pains are not yet wholly alleviated, the following aspect of 3QO will aid in your deliverance. The barely perceivable quantum highly improbable option that lies on the right side of the moat comes with the burgeoning wisdom that pain is a phenomenon that exists far beneath all the guilt and blame-encrusted, insulting explanations we attribute to it. While this book will later make clearer how pain existed before humanity had even sprung from the celestial loins, for now just do the best you can to strip the insults off the injury. With each breath, attempt to feel the pain as a straightforward and pure sensation (as unpleasant as it experientially is), and turn your mind's insulting explanations for the pain into gibberish. Start by saying your logical mind's reason for the ordeal, and then progress into playfully turning these words into a hodgepodge of sound. See this word porridge as industrial-strength soap and your aching sensations as bits of sludge about to be emulsified and sucked down this right-side drain into a new river, then a new ocean. Imagine this new ocean, if you can, as being a relatively empty corner in the belly of God. Your capacity to allow pain as something needing no accouterment of insults, truly breaks down this glop into food for the Gods. And by the way, those endorphins are pumping, and your pain is diminishing.

17. Let's bring it all home. Once upon a time, you experienced pain that indeed did overwhelm you. The devastating thoughts and emotions that arose in response to the unbearable sensations buried themselves in your subconscious, along with the corporeal contractions. They were stored there waiting for a time that as an adult you might bring them back up to be healed, resolved, and understood. So, heck, you're doing it now. "You were only waiting for this moment to arrive." The jig is up, the story can be put to pasture, and all the defeat surrounding your agony is being alchemized into victory. Count from ten slowly backward to one. At ten you are allowed to believe still the story that your childhood pains made you a *victim*. See the *victim* at ten and the *victor* at one. What a beautiful job you are truly doing. Ten, nine, eight, seven, six, five, four, three, two, one …

Chapter 6

Anxiety and Depression

As the appellation of this text implies, injured feelings and mental suffering can be substantially relieved by subtracting a mountain of salt your mind has caustically employed to season your emotional wounds. Whatever traumas you've experienced (as utterly wrenching as they were at the time), the destructive manner in which you presently frame them is patently flawed. It is the result of repeated ancient conclusions unconsciously continuing to steer your emotive ship. These ageless judgments once served as executive proclamations your brain used to sum up overwhelmingly adverse sensations. At that time, the mind was rightly compelled to determine how every given trauma negatively altered a complex set of survivability indices stored in the brain. Evolution had guided us to *experience* life in our gut and heart, yet *evaluate* it in our minds. This prefrontal mind assessor's design arose to 'chop-chop' appraise complex issues and to then make rapid executive orders for the rest of our being to abide.

Oh, yes, many thousands of years ago, our prefrontal cortex was the absolute bomb. If it rocked, we rolled, and it rarely made errors. When it said, "Dummy, if you go to the watering hole first thing in the morning, you're gonna get eaten," well by gosh, it was best to pin your ears back and take heed. It extracted the phenomenon of fear out of the purely bio-physiologic realm of other mammals and turned it into a premeditated warning/reasoning voice in our minds. At its earliest stages, that voice proffered blatant forewarnings about immediate possibilities of pending death and how to maximize the probability to circumvent said demise. As the arrangement later became more refined, more subtle, and more understated, executive formulations were articulated to be amplified via the voice. This survival-enhancing sector of the brain in due course fittingly surmised that we had grown sufficiently accustomed to obeying imminent life and death directives, and were ready to turn our attention toward evaluating more conceptual, less impending matters about long-term survivability. This more ultimate vision included inner voice guidelines that would deal with the intricacies of mating and an entire array of newly complicated foci for the mind to mull over.

As previously stated, these more abstract issues pertained to an individual's survival prospects concerning his given community. The viability of primitive societies decisively rested upon the strengths and gifts of all its members to maximize surviving attacks by other tribes, periodic food shortages, epidemics, and a myriad of other portentous misfortunes. If an individual were to fall below some imperceptible line of delineation, where their minimal semblance of usefulness to the community was in question, Darwinian survival burdens could force a tribe to remove the chaff from the wheat. In other words, don't let the cave door slam as you leave and become food for some saber-toothed pussycat. So, while the neo-cortex continued to cover the obvious, "Don't collect berries over there; the mastodons are eating there now," it began to more broadly recognize that you were just as likely to be chaff purposefully winnowed from your tribe as accidentally succumbing to a predator. And while overt dangers had become relatively predictable, the obtuse range of subtleties about one's worth to their community was a near constant stress-inducing perplexity. And while we previously tackled how this ceaseless worry permanently interfered with endorphin response and physical pain relief, we will now examine the emotional mayhem born of the same riddle.

As evolutionarily substantial as the neo-cortex had been in the longevity of the species, its techniques for getting our attention and promulgating its intent were extraordinarily monotonic. Its stringing together of thoughts and their bio-chemical dugout boats that traveled from neuron to neuron to alert us to act in such a way as to avoid cataclysmic danger, relied on a scant few neurotransmitters. In this way, our minds did not have to incessantly reinvent the wheel but depended on those old hands, the mammalian fight, fright, and flight compounds, adrenaline and cortisol. These substances made in the body alert biological systems to act upon the executive order that danger is to be dealt with posthaste. To guarantee swift and efficient reactions to maximize survivability, they operate in a cyclic manner. A fear-inducing thought begets the chemicals; and then the increasing fear neurotransmitters in the bloodstream alert the neo-cortex and nudge it to reinforce the idea, which then calls for more chemicals that trumpet ever louder the body's need to react decisively.

It is noteworthy that these very same substances that flowed in reaction to life-and-death thoughts would later serve as well to light a fire under us if we lagged behind in our obligations to the tribe. And yet here we are, thousands of years later, beating this same old dead horse. A predominant percentage of the emotional stressors weakening our inner balance arise from these utterly obsolete and ninety-nine percent past their due date, archetypally entrenched tribal fears. Abandonment issues categorically do not originate (as Freud was wont to obsess), as neurotic reactions to all our parents' fiascos and failures. They arose eons ago in nuanced true-to-life and death anguish. Will the tribe support us through our time of trial, or will it frankly abandon us and benefit from our death? Ouch ... cold. Through neural pathways that Carl Jung calls collective unconscious archetypes, the reliving of this entrenched memory, this ultimate insult added to injury, happens to most of us sometimes, and some of us most of the time. And though I will examine the bottomless well of romantic angst in a later chapter, the tribe frankly benefited from us most when we were in fulfilling and functional romances. The depth of failure and fear that presently accompanies romantic heartbreak absolutely occurs as the archetypal memory rises in us that the tribe got quite discouraged with the moping that went with relationship failure. We humans are quite driven therefore to assure everyone we know how good our romances are doing. And when they fail (as so many sadly do), we sure as heck are going to blame it on the other person, so the tribe doesn't abandon us as if we are useless lovers doomed to nosedive in whatever relationship follows.

In this dominion of emotional and mental suffering, I will distill our dialogue down to the energetic core bottleneck affecting a majority of mental health patients. This archetypal neurotransmitter boondoggle straps us into a seesaw of existence, primarily expressed as depression or anxiety. Let's imagine that you have been in a relationship that is ending or perhaps just going through a rough stretch. In and of itself, this would tend to only briefly open sad, intense feelings in your gut, which would cause you to function more slowly for a forlorn but reasonable period. We all know the weighty feeling. There is absolutely no tangible, immediate threat to your existence. Except, no one ever alerted the neo-cortex to stand down and stop micromanaging our very survivable present-day emotional hurts. When our early ancestors lost a mate, and the leaden feeling settled in their guts, after a reasonable period of inner healing, the enteric nervous system permeated their systems with a stimulating mild cocktail of adrenaline and cortisol. Otherwise, if they mourned their lost love too long, they risked banishment from the tribe because of lingering inactivity. If the ancient grief was too strong though, perhaps a surviving or abandoned mate eternally lost their zest for life. Feasibly they stopped caring for so long that they were tied to a tree so an animal would devour them and free their tribe from the burden of maintaining the upkeep for a suddenly useless member. But how long was too long, and who could ever have been astute enough to measure all the subtle looming scenarios playing upon a particular tribe in any given moment? Could one's last words have been, "Don't drive me out. I just need two more days, and I'll be a chipper cave-boy again".

These ageless enigmatic memories drift down old carved riverbeds, lugging ancient chemical imprints of threatened survival into today's feelings of sadness. What should otherwise be a relatively short period where our instinctive, dark reaction to lost love inhibits our sociability, instead is liable to turn into a mini-calamity. If the dense energy inhabiting your alimentary canal were allowed to navigate without erroneous neo-cortex alarm, one hundred million very astute enteric neurons would activate all the serotonin residing in your solar plexus, and a natural and profound emotive healing would in due course occur. Instead, the emotive havoc, a unicycle of single-minded negativity, breeds its metastatic madness. Fearing, as it does, that this dense energy leads to social withdrawal, which leads to expulsion, the unconscious repeats ancient judgments of impending banishment and abandonment. It first attempts to numb and escape this alarming and impending doom, pressing it down into a depressurized zone we intuitively refer to as depression. With this state causing, in turn, a counterbalancing of panic, the body inundates the system with adrenaline and cortisol, which replace dense gut feelings with fight, fright, and flight floods of fear and anxiety. So instead of the enteric nervous system slowly and naturally healing its weightiness with mild adrenaline/cortisol and generous scoops of serotonin and dopamine, the gut is left in suspended animation, as anxiety and fear trumpet the advance of yet another unidentifiable threat.

The venomous sequence that ensues is that the heaviness or pressure in your gut lays unattended in the onslaught of fear chemicals demanding fight or flight. Because it is denied the healing 'happy chemicals' trumped by the neo-cortex's belief that fighting possible societal banishment and death requires healing to take a backseat, a double physiologic whammy supervenes. Meanwhile, the unconscious demands higher and higher levels of anxiety-increasing adrenaline to combat the initial life-threatening weight of emotional separation/mini-death, and secondly the paralysis of encroaching depression. While depression and anxiety can sometimes appear to be symptomatic of two very opposite emotional and mental maladies, we have just seen how they are a veritable Mississippi two-step, each egging the other on with wicked indomitability.

Though Jung's collective unconscious archetypes predetermine in each of us these present permutations of emotional upset, we are also each supremely capable of witnessing these destructive involuntary calibrations and gaining sovereignty to alter them. To begin to access this self-determination, you are not required to accept my theory about *Darwinian tribal exclusion* fears. What you must acknowledge, however, is that the two predominant gut sensations, depression and anxiety, are waiting to be viewed through a state-of-the-art, cutting-edge lens. That lens is your conscious will, your birthright, and your fortitude to use your life as an exercise in freedom from the shackles of complacent normality. So whether your anxiety and depression are garden variety mild to moderate subclinical sensations that most of us experience as merely "kind of a drag," or are severe diagnosable conditions worthy of medication and psychotherapy, there is a simple understanding here that can thoroughly alter your life.

If your gut sensation falls under the category of anxiety,

assign your mind the dual task of paying attention to the physical experience while you are simultaneously recognizing the negative assessment your mind is ascribing to the sensation. As stated above, fear is a cyclical vortex that operates by sensations begetting thoughts generating fear neurotransmitters and so on and so on. In the one percent of the time that your anxiety is a well-founded component of an appropriate fear cycle, the thoughts and sensations and chemicals are all properly in sync. And yet as stated throughout this book, ninety-nine percent of the fear thoughts your mind is using to spur on insults to your injuries is part of a specious, vestigial computer program requiring updating. So notice how the physical sensation of anxiety is unpleasant and annoying, but in of itself, it is certainly far less daunting than the negative story you are reflexively weaving through it. Take a deep breath and remind your mind that its assumption of the gut fluttering being a sign that something dreadful is about to go down is an old, erroneous transpersonal movie script. It is a computer virus and can with effort be updated by the mere aptitude your mind has to remind itself that in and of itself, gut fluttering is but a sign of *energy bubbling to life*. I get it; you have spent the better part of your lifetime doing everything in your power to modulate, control, or entirely suppress this effervescence. But this is the time to change, and you can gradually experience yourself inviting the dynamism to come forth more lightly. Bring inner sound or dance or a vision of an inner painting into your heart-scape, using this energy formerly known as *anxiety* as the fuel of an expanding you. In truth, in the natural biological cycle, cortisol is at its highest daily levels about a half hour after we awaken. This is so we might use its awakening properties to sufficiently rouse us out of the sleep state and into the functioning that our days insist we address. And yet our Starbucks stockholders can rest easy, for that gush of cortisol is usually met with apprehension, as if this natural 'upper' signifies something frightening is about to happen. So we awaken, suppress the cortisol, and promptly need some coffee to wake us up instead.

When cortisol, formerly demonized as a signal of anxiety, is in measured perfection, your gut/soul is taking its rightful place at the helm of the ship your ego used to navigate through the fearful, choppy waters of its self-manufactured horror movie. This dynamism, arising from the enteric one hundred million neurons strong real you, will fuel your existence to become more full of grace. Scream yes over and over until every cell in your body perks up its periscopic little ears and hears the truth. Let freedom ring.

If your unpleasant gut sensation is not the deluging rising of energy formerly known as anxiety, it is by and large the empty pit or imploding weightiness we *en regle generale* vilify as depression. Fortunately, just as we have effectuated with anxiety, we are about to reframe, rename, and reclaim this seemingly monolithic negative bottomless well. Depression is the numbing deadening feeling that we sadly create in our gut/soul in aversion to the natural pressure that is meant to simmer like lava from our solar plexuses. As explained throughout this book, the pressurized yin fragment of the primordial compression is habitually misconstrued and dreaded. We have thus spent an entire lifetime listening to society brainwashing us into "lightening up." We live with this incremental denial and guilt surrounding the naturally dense pressure of our real souls. All we manage to do through this rejection of heaviness is creating an even more depressurized emptiness in our gut. With our depressurization successful, we are left with vaster realms of depression. (Yes, I have over-emphasized this in order to thoroughly punctuate the way we create our own depression.)

And as we have accomplished in taking wisdom's wrecking ball to the haunted house of anxiety, so have we also done in applying some shrewd new insights to emulsify the prison cell we slavishly allow depression to lock us in. We do not *get* depressed or *have* depression; we press down on our gut/soul energies and *create* depression. And the instant you understand that and go inside your own body and tell your enteric one hundred million neurons that their weight is worthy, depression will promptly begin healing and entering into its launch to become life-fuel.

Chapter 7

Issues and Personality Disorders

As opposed to the gut sensation glitches associated with the mood disorders (depression and anxiety), personality disorders are defined by behaviors that differ starkly from societal norms and expectations. Take for instance a hypothetical braggart leader whom others may consider has a narcissistic personality disorder, yet who himself feels eminently satisfied with his behavior. So whereas mood disorders always cause suffering to those afflicted, personality disordered people occasionally cause more suffering to others than themselves. Narcissists in particular habitually cling self-adoringly to their disorders, while those who suffer from other personality syndromes such, as borderline personality disorder or obsessive-compulsive disorder, generally angst and seek psychological counseling.

The crucial crux to behold is that on the continuum known as humanity, most of us living in Western civilization exhibit mild to moderate chunks of subclinical personality disorder almost daily. Most of us live with a singularly unique encoded subconscious swamp, replete with quicksand, sinkholes, poisonous snakes, booby traps, issues, triggers, pet peeves, martyred stories, Pandora's boxes, Achilles' heels, and … have I mentioned issues yet? Alas, even many of us stalwart spiritual seekers, investing precious time and treasure to slough our burdensome egos, inadvertently preserve a few prized martyred issues caged beneath the veneer of our transcendent personas.

Conceivably, the most ubiquitous sentiment on the entire planet fits into the broad-spectrum span of "you wantonly hurt my feelings." This ranges all the way from subtle variants of "you made me sad," or "you made me angry," to the blatant hatreds and prejudices that color humanity's psychic and physical wars against those who appear superficially dissimilar from them. This cozy blanket of blame and finger pointing virtually stretches all across the mental health continuum, warming the cold, isolated soul landscapes where we would all otherwise have to rise and *heal* our own subconscious pains. Thus, some of the pathognomonic diagnostic indicators of narcissism and borderline personality disorder incongruously extend to include just about all of us. As we societally remain eminently content to rationalize the fine art of allocating fault for our emotional pains as a justifiable cast-iron paradigm, how can we deign to suggest that personality disordered individuals should forfeit their king-size portions of blame-hurling?

Why do emotional pain and blame feel so darn cozy together, kind of like hot fudge and ice cream, windy spring days and kite flying, and July 4th and barbeques? We'll explore. As the word *subconscious* implies, it's like having a vast subfloor or basement warehouse where the conscious mind can store an unlimited expanse of sensorial memories. And while the smell of Grandma's home-baked scones might pop up now and again from this subterranean jurisdiction, the term *subconscious* first and foremost is uttered as psychotherapists deliberate their patients' emotional and mental duress. As to why we need this warehouse, obliged to spend our lives toting around negative imprints of each unpleasant moment we have experienced, the answer is both bittersweet and downright sad. Isn't it quite forlorn enough that traumas occurred in the first place? What kind of evenhandedness can the universe have, that we are beholden to store reminiscences of these ordeals such that every time the basement floods, the morbid carcasses rise back up to the ground floor to be re-experienced in one neurotic categorization or another?

In accordance with the entire leitmotif of this book, I will demonstrate why it was once necessary for this unconscious tangle to transpire. I will establish how the subconscious mind was part and parcel of the prehistoric grounds for our survival. And when I am finished, and together we forgive cosmic consciousness for the necessary evil these subliminal concentrations have wrought, I will clarify how we arise at this juncture as free as possible to delete most of this worthless crap from our minds. I mean it, as ripe and juicy for change as we ever have been as a species. Drumroll, maestro.

There was a pregnant moment in the history of this planet when the human mind stretched past its mammalian and reptilian boundaries and glimpsed the boundless possibilities of creative, moment-to-moment cognizance. Rather than lingering in limbo, limited to a handful of automatic animal instincts that arose predominantly in perilous circumstances, the human neo-cortex awoke us to an evolving capacity to formulate up-to-the-minute responses in the face of radically emergent events. This nascent ability to not only devise strategies but to also create weapons, tools, and rudimentary conveniences was a turning point in the antediluvian bloom of the human flower. We survived because we thought. Descartes might have been late to the game in his calling a spade a spade, but "I think therefore I am" just about nailed it. Much bigger, stronger, nastier, and gnarlier species have permanently exited the earth drama, stage left. But despite a few unique self-defeating habits humans continue to exhibit, this thinking on our feet talent carried the day. And we are still here.

And if one of us spaced out back in those white-knuckle

times and stopped using his head for a moment, one could only hope that the bungle was not lethal but merely bumpy. And if the bumbler was thus blessed to live another day, you can bet his neo-cortex had a slice of negative feedback to reinforce the perception that the next oversight would be lethal. "In fact, Dopey," the vainglorious neo-cortex relentlessly harangued, "if you're too stupid to remain vigilant at all times, I'm going to engrave a semi-permanent imprint in the back of your mind that you have to carry whether you like it or not." This subfloor of mental and emotional inscriptions had a dual function that made it an ideal component of individual and species-wide survival. First, this neural engraving served to immunize one from an immediate commensurate future danger spawning a similar life-threatening lapse. Second, the queasy memory of near demise would sit in our subconscious, urging us and gnawing at us from within to develop evolving mental skills. It was like homework, an assignment that forced us to intelligently advance. Good deal, huh?

And the grace of elongating time into a blessing was no small matter. Indeed, in circumstances where we had nearly paid the ultimate price for our slipup, we most likely were in no shape to immediately analyze our faux pas. We likely had both physical and emotional wounds to lick. But later, in the coming days, weeks, or months, that nauseating picture of the moment of near demise would arise into our mindscape and re-scold us as to how vulnerable our oversight had made us. Ideally, we would use this reawakened memory to determine all the skills we could develop that inoculated us not only from the same danger but from analogous jeopardies we had never encountered before. Once we were confident in this evaluation, the memory could be safely deleted from our unconscious. But ...

Oh yes, the pervasive 'but.' As humans became self-aware of the precarious nature of calculations and subsequent actions demarcating our tightrope walk between life and death, we understandably lost the guiltlessness and guilelessness of animal nature. Rather than being content to follow pure survival instincts as animals do, we humans began to brood about our occasional mental missteps. And frankly, sometimes there were just such copious amounts of challenges to surmount in the present, that those damn subconscious memories of near-death errors on our part just had to freakin' wait.

And in that time of waiting, our plights that till then had principally been within ourselves, morphed into a whole new world of interpersonal emotional mayhem. As pointed out earlier, Darwinian survival odds had changed at some juncture from an individual's battle against the elements into a cooperative tribal tapestry of interrelated moving parts. Over time, each member of a tribal group grew more and more mindful of who around them swelled the odds of their continued existence, and bluntly, who was a slight or worse drag on the tribe. Even as subtle a sign as the stride of a formerly confident person progressively devolving into a gait that broadcast trepidation, alerted tribal members to one's mounting lack of confidence. Or an odor of fear might alert the nostrils of one's cohorts that self-confidence no longer biochemically operated his physiology. As they sniffed this apprehension and began to demonstrably lose confidence in you, your fear of banishment compounded subconscious worries, and frankly, the sweating one was screwed. Where were those early start-up deodorant companies when you needed one?

In this torrent of inner turmoil, the tree of thought could bear countless forms of rotten fruit. One, of course, would be apt to entertain anguished beliefs as fellow tribe members increasingly beheld you as a weak link in their survival chain. Furthermore, one was likely to feel victimized by the condescending countenances of others. "I was feeling relatively good until Caveman X looked at me like I'm some sort of loser. Now, damn it, I'm feeling and consequently looking exceedingly threatened." (Poor Jeb Bush.) And as the nuances of tribal membership grew ever more convoluted with possible ulterior motives to ban a familial colleague, a thousand permutations of warranted and un-warranted mistrusts cluttered the halls of the subconscious storage room with metastatic unremittingness.

Suffice it to say that all these thousands of years later, nearly every individual now walking the earth is engorged with enough personal and old Jungian transpersonal dreads and qualms in their subconscious that the spring-loaded mousetrap of their mind is hair-triggered to go off at the slightest provocation. So when someone either says or does something slightly or moderately offensive (or we imagine that they do), layers of repressed subconscious fear and pain begin to break free from the psychic storage room. And when that trigger goes off, and the subliminal mind dredges up the old threatened survival thick sludge in our soul/gut, we wrap the lava dripping over the levee with our pet pre-arranged ribbons. This bow will be one of a handful of whatever martyred, angry, or resentful insults our minds have grown accustomed to using to explain the habituated heartrending emotion to our egos. And even though the insult added to the injury erroneously codifies the feeling as if it is happening in the present through the ill will of another, the ego finds consolation. This bizarre comfort in the victim-laden rhetoric we bathe ourselves in is because by putting a ribbon on our box full of pain, our egos are free to believe that with vigilance we will outsmart and protect ourselves from the proverbial bad guys. And in no way do we feel forced or compelled to examine the contours or the vastness of any painful emotion. We have swathed ourselves in the old Darwinian comfort of blame and utter non-responsibility. Ah, that ignorant bliss. That the emotional angst and fear are merely old transpersonal subconscious memories that could be processed and released at the snap of our fingers escapes our humorless egos.

If you feel ready to subtract these issues and triggers

and semi-personality disordered BS (belief systems) from your psychic repertoire, let's have a go at it. As I have stated previously, this may not be exactly *easy*, but it is incredibly *simple*. When you feel wronged, and your lawyer ego builds its case and presents its damning facts, be the higher judge and dismiss the charges. That's right—dismiss it, darn it. Case closed. And once you have, the next step emerges, which is that your gut will feel uncomfortable. When that happens, you become liberated to feel and subsequently release the deeper fears that were attached to your visceral discomfort. You probably don't remember accidentally walking into that mastodon feeding area and nearly being killed and realizing what a weak idiot you were and how the next time you wouldn't be so lucky to survive. As well, you don't likely recall being forced from your tribe twenty thousand years ago. More to be expected, you might hark back to feeling hurt as a child and declaring to yourself that one day you wouldn't be so vulnerable to others' insensitivity. Whether or not any memories arise after the judge dismisses the case, you are welcome to realize and declare to yourself that whatever weighty sensation you are presently feeling in your gut, if you do nothing except observe it and breathe through it, it will begin to heal. There is no longer any advantage to mulling over past mistakes. The energy is arising to be rehabilitated, and all you have to do to accomplish this is follow my handy little rhyme. First, we conceal it, and then we reveal it, so we can feel it and routinely heal it. That's right—if you subtract all insult from the injury, the dense sensation in your gut will automatically begin to heal—and quickly at that. You just stop believing the martyred, angry, accusatory words you are attaching in the present to the very unpleasant feeling in your gut. Then you are free to realize that any unconscious Darwinian or old personal feelings attached to the heaviness no longer have any need to be examined. None. So the sensation that was buried long ago to warn you that you were too vulnerable has no remaining reason to hang out in your gut. It releases, and you can suddenly breathe more fully.

And it is more than fine if this long-standing habit of blaming others for your hurts takes a moment or two for you to divest yourself of entirely. If initially you dissolve your flame-throwing blame-thrower every other time, that would be awesome. Two out of three times—wow, you're almost a pro. Combining mind/body medicine and significant spiritual growth … Yeah, you are becoming your own guru. Go for it.

Chapter 8

Subtracting Relationship Insults

Rarely is the malignant repartee of insults raining down upon injuries so bald-facedly misbegotten as it is in the tunnel of romantic love. In this aberrational, imperfect storm of a fool's golden opportunity, the initial intoxicating aroma of Eros invites a smorgasbord of disconsolate childhood disenchantments up from the brooding caverns of our subconscious. In a dream garden of bait and switch, these feelings arise, we surmise, gloriously to be mended at last. For is not the subliminal inference of romance such that our beloved has finally arrived to kiss the sleeping beauty of our moribund emotional hope? Was not the broken, limping journey to this very moment of our newest passion ritual only bearable because it was subliminally foretold that Prince/Princess Charming would materialize to cauterize the bleeding disappointments of our childhood? Was not Paul McCartney channeling our deepest heart when he sang, "All your life, you were only waiting for this moment to arise"? And most crucially, were not the wretched emotional cruelties or oversights of our parents just sticking in God's craw until he could ultimately make it up to us by presenting us our perfect Beloved?

Ah, but how hastily we in due course rappel down from the mountaintop of ecstasy, only to end up in the Grand Canyon of the most caustic romantic blame. Instead of the miracle cure of love that our petulant subconscious assumed was God's quid pro quo for us agreeing to survive our woeful childhoods, the dormant volcano egged on by the archetypal white lie of ardor is now multiplying our sorrows to the max. Oh, the plot distinctly thickens in these *Hunger Games* of love. Whereas our everyday guilt and fear-ridden interplay with physical and emotional angst have been expounded upon earlier, this uniquely penetrating interaction with a love interest brings a matchless, explicitly atrocious set of unconscious precepts to the table.

While a sweeping sense of assumed justified martyrdom pushes us daily to blame others for garden variety emotional upsets, the specific venomous denunciation we reserve for our fallen beloveds necessitates its own elucidation. And this time, we need not venture solely back to our cave-dwelling, Darwinian forebears for the clarity required to gain the proficiency to subtract insult from romantic injuries. The scent of this contorted miasma munificently flowing into the bank accounts of divorce lawyers and marriage counselors, wafts back much closer to home, to our own childhood (where else, eh, Sigmund?). Hence, it is requisite that we examine the two pillars of childhood illusion that created a double helix of bound juvenile resentment. This headwater of umbrage that sits in our unconscious waiting to be healed by our fairy tale Beloved, eventually unravels and emerges as a two-fisted body punch to romance.

The first pillar of infantile illusion is the false promise of archetypal, absolute maternal (and to a lesser extent, paternal) fealty and fortification against all childhood pains. As Eve was biblically hung on the semantic cross of "bearing children to multiply her sorrow," so it was thus ordained as the exemplar that mothers would feel both responsibility and guilt concerning their children's pains. With baby books, bottles, breasts, and beatifically blissful intentions, Mom projects to her offspring this warranty that she will perform as biblically advertised. Despite her noble objectives, this prearranged illusion had zero possibilities of proving correct. Alas, the gravity of truth collapsed this fabrication, and life was confirmed to have a darker palette than Disney-inspired fantasies attempted to fortify. And when the great maternal ignis fatuus crumbled under the weight of truth, our childhood nervous systems were loath to embrace the disillusionment in one fell swoop. Today, if we're remotely prepared to pass from ignorant bliss into realms where truth hurts and courageously remain un-benumbed there long enough for the truth to set us free, we might taste the fruits of evolution. We sure as heck weren't ready to do this as toddlers.

No, instead when Mom and Dad fizzled as absolute protectors against our natural pains of being incarnate organisms, we were wholly unprepared. Without the physiologic capacity at that age to ferment in the realm where the truth hurts, we were also unable to return to the illusory parental protective omnipotence. What to do? Life sure as hell couldn't have an entire species of crushed spirits on its hands. So fresh from the pillowy tufts of Cupid's white wings, fluttered the next fairytale, a brand new ignorant bliss all our own! And though, quite frankly, this new emperor was as starkly naked as the old one, beggars could not be choosers.

A romantic promissory note entitling us to 'the one and only' would arrive in what was for us a sprouting new realm of time; the future. For rather than dimming the light of hope and recognizing that our parents' failures to vaccinate us against pain represented reality, we were given a guaranteed winning lottery ticket to future love. Instead of drowning in the depth of our gut/soul/id when our parental lifeguards proved they weren't swimmers themselves, we were formulated to store disappointments in the hard drives of our subconscious minds. There, every overwhelming childhood sensation could be filed away with a crucial caveat that allowed ignorant bliss to survive. That stipulation was that our parents' failure to protect and love us as we were promised was not the objective truth of humanity but rather was their personal shortcoming. We frankly just did not have the gumption yet to see it as an overall reflection of the tangible limitations of humankind. And so, even the most crushing sensations of disenchantment were stored away, folded neatly into the emperor's wardrobe, with the sustaining belief that if not for the screwed-up defects of our parents, we wouldn't have had to suffer the pains of childhood. And consequently, when we were old enough to escape the imperfect world of these flawed parental units, we would automatically be in line to meet the mates we so richly deserved. Oh yeah!

The second illusion, the grand dame of all human neuroses, is the Oedipal and Electra complex. This multifarious confluence of hang-ups provides the piece de resistance for the banquet of bitter pills we will swallow through life's entire romantic pilgrimage. Popular culture would have us believe that the primary attraction of the opposite sex is a glamorous pursuit for the chic qualities of our paramour. Let's look squarely at what more gravely bespeaks the core of desperation agitating us toward romantic pain relief. When a child experiences infantile intoxicating liberation from the pains in their Id (discomfort in the gut), through the affections and energy fields of the opposite-gendered parent, the Oedipal/Electra complex surreptitiously coopts a significant share of the subconscious drives that will shape their entire life. As to why and how the transpersonal yin-charged particles of a little girl and the yang-charged particles of a little boy are infinitely comforted by the polarity in their gender-opposite parent, a later chapter will elucidate this in greater detail. For now, I will only say that when peered at through the global lens of all creatures mating, the birds and the bees is as fundamental a dynamic as gravity, magnetism, and the unyielding expansion of the physical universe.

I advocate that the crestfallen disenchantment and frustration at the core of the Oedipal/Electra kerfuffle was designed by the infinite consciousness as part of the institutionalized ignorant bliss. This means that all the jealousy and romantic insecurity that arises beginning in puberty as a result of the early sexual magnetism and subsequent rejection toddlers experienced with their opposite-gendered parent was part and parcel of keeping us greyhounds chasing mechanical rabbits around the racetrack. As a baby boy feeling energetic release and pleasure through the sexual polarity between myself and my mother, her seeming rejection of me and bedding of my father becomes an agony. His jealousy of her attention to me compounds the mess. It will all fuel my teenage and adult lusts, making me driven to conquer later surrogate mothers and overcome perceived surrogate fathers. This lifelong competition will foment my machismo, which, as we will see in a later chapter, is tragically vital to our cosmic puzzle.

If lovers can distinguish that a vast preponderance of the issues arising in their romance has so very little to do with *the now*, the drumbeat of cosmic alchemy can invite them into mystery's amphitheater to beat the tympani of quantum healing. Whether through same-sex union or hetero amalgamation, this non-egoistic opportunity for yin and yang to use lovers to eventuate the creation of sacred substance, makes the Odyssey into the ocean of amorousness worth the gamble for those so inclined. Despite the emotional obstacle course that will demand its pound of flesh from you, I highly recommend it.

CHAPTER 9

Sealing Imprisoned False Ceilings

Carl Jung's insights on the collective unconscious of humankind paved a broad, unique pathway for characterizing the complexities of our species. While most therapists still, as a rule, dissect and analyze an individual's behaviors, attitudes, actions, thoughts, feelings, neuroses, and psychoses, Jung's genius regarding the shared transpersonal dynamic of the human mind is still far too overlooked. As a profession, psychology has spent so much effort postulating about how and why the poor 'sickos' have fallen from our comforting cocoon orb of normalness that we have entirely overlooked the possibility that our routine collective psychic machinery is, in of itself, a shattered, id-strangled mechanism. The human proclivity toward constructing personalized inferences about our deeply seated intractable snags keeps us erecting injurious, dualistic paradigms. A prominent one is that the pathetic non-sane populace are suffering, while those of us who have no psychopathology reside in a high-quality place where sanity holds us against its munificent breast.

Of course, countless other boundless sages besides Jung have confronted the facileness of the human sheep bleating out their unexamined 'ego thought'. In Dostoevsky's novel *The Idiot,* the id-infused idiocy and non-sanity of the main character,

Prince Lev Nikolayevich Myshkin, is attributed more to his depth, honesty, trustfulness, kindness, and humility than to any dearth of intellectual ability. Furthermore, Nietzsche claimed, in his *The Antichrist,* that Jesus was insane because, in his id-bathed soul, he had an aversion toward the material world. So too back in Shakespearian times, the character of the *fool* often conveyed the core of truth that 'normal' characters were averse to personifying. And modern culture continually provides us stories of characters who are initially portrayed as crazy, only to reveal in the theatrical denouement that they possess some perception that far surpasses the conventional realm of sanity.

As the incidence of psychopathology inexorably spirals out of control, I consider it wise for us to question whether the very state of being we deem to be sane is not itself a tourniquet, tightly bound around a dysfunctional id-starved collective mind-form. From the Latin root *sanus,* which means 'healthy', comes the word *sanity*. Bloated with Western civilization's dubitable values, sanity is a concept fraught with the oxymoronic inferences of post-modern crassness. Let us observe two men walking separately into the psych ward of a well-regarded hospital. Greg Kilman is homeless, dressed in tattered clothing, and unwashed. He is muttering incoherently about the end of the world and the corporate greed that is speeding us toward this unavoidable expiration date. He is certifiably diagnosable as existing far outside our sanitized *sanus* and accordingly diagnosed and medicated. The second man, dressed in a dapper suit, shares a name with this wing of the hospital he is visiting today to receive an award for his philanthropy. This is Winston Jameson, who donated three and a half million dollars to help finance the creation of the Winston Jameson Psychiatric Center. His toothy grin and charismatic walk say it all. If his sanity could be bottled, it would sell for thousands per amulet. Jameson Armaments is by far the area's principal local employer. Just the fact that its salesmen troll the mansions of third-world despots who seek these weapons to kill those who thrust towards the grace of liberty is not to be weighed on the scales where sanity or the lack thereof is apportioned. Kony and his drugged child soldier minions, particularly admire Jameson's new and improved line of shiny semiautomatics. ISIS swoons for the semis as well, though their mullahs insist that they capture the weapons rather than having to spend cold cash themselves.

After receiving his award, Jameson plans to head straight to the country club for golf with his best buddy, Stan Reynolds, who also employs countless locals and donates generously to worthy charities as well. Reynolds makes his fortune killing with cigarettes those who are not blown apart by Winnie's guns. Today they'll be joined by Rod Forrest, who owns the hottest bar and nightclub in the city. The golf buddies often joke about how many parking spots Rod's establishment is required *by law* to maintain, considering that our sane society forbids drinking and driving. Relatively few of those who park at Rod's and other bars all across America kill and maim innocent people while driving home drunk, so who am I to be a killjoy? The sane people write the laws, after all, and when the music stops, the objective pain has to take its bite out of somebody.

And so, employing Jung's perspicacity regarding the impersonal nature of archetypes, we are liberated to examine whether sanity is merely a collective false ceiling under which people have been programmed to live. The why of this proposition is back to our general theme of humanity's need for ignorant bliss. The wherefore of the collective false ceiling is as follows: Every human babe in arms, regardless of specific details, is born into a generalized state of helplessness. An infant's very first primal experience is having the entirety of its existence dependent on others who universally perform functions that the newborn itself can't. Though not initially coded in worded thought forms, defeated feelings permeate the gut. "I can't walk, talk, read, feed myself, change my own diaper, medicate my pain, or in any form do anything to relieve my own situation, but everyone else around me seems to be doing all of those things with eminent efficiency. The first primal answer then to my pain as an infant is; "I am pathetic and helpless, but luckily, everyone else is not."

Though it is indeed a bummer that our primal human experience is an abject and unique sense of helplessness, at least the secondary immediate archetype of our parents' slavish obedience to relieve our pains should count for something. But alas, this second archetype is hardly a blessing and rather constitutes the initial framework of our human false ceiling. If there had been words in these early times, they would have roughly been, "I have pain and need for relief. I cannot myself do anything to relieve my own suffering. It appears, however, that all these other beings in my life not only can help me, but if I cry loud enough, they seem to have every inclination to rush to my service." Considering what a detriment our primal helplessness would be to an eventual blossoming of our species, the early assuaging archetypal false ceiling of the belief that at least all our pains will be attended to promptly is a paramount bedrock of collective human unconscious.

By 'false ceiling', I am implying that no matter how much psychic or physical pain I am experiencing in a situation, the standard state of affairs would be that most of the other humans are out of pain (and hence aware that they should be doing everything possible to heal *me*). The false ceiling demands us to explain every un-full aspect of our cup of life as a mistake. In other words, our default expectation is that if everything goes as it should go, there will be only momentary pain that will be relieved by others. Again, the primal helplessness attached to our first pains was only bearable with this nearly immediate sense that others would automatically attend to our every angst. Ever see a human acting as if he were entitled to be taken care of? *Ever see one who didn't?* (Thank heavens there are a few!) Ever see a chronic pain patient hating a medical practitioner who implied that a lower dose of pain medicine would be healthier?

The false ceiling is so all-encompassing in all interactions with others and ourselves that it has become the essential fabric of human thought. I may be struggling, but as long as the collective unconscious memory of parental duty to the abatement of my pain pervades my unconscious attitude, I can believe that help is just a moment away. Of course, Freud supplied humanity with a sponge that absorbed much of the pain that inevitably spills out of the perfect hope of the false ceiling archetype. Get your box of Kleenex ready. Freud, by and large, gave humanity a protocol by which an individual can have their cake and eat it too. Let me digress (my apologies of course that my writing style is often one hanging participle of a digression after another).

If the false ceiling is the collective unconscious first antidote for the newborn's primordial perception of pain and helplessness, what do children do a little later in their young lives when they initially cognize that all the king's horses and all the king's men, aren't putting them together again? In other words, in the continuum of *I experience pain, I am helpless to alleviate my own suffering,* but *all those around me seem able and inclined to ease my pain,* what thoughts and feelings occur inside me when a number of my early pains begin to fall through the cracks of this tidy paradigm? I have often witnessed as a child falls and hurts himself slightly, the child whimpers and looks up at his mother accusingly. The timbre of the child's accompanying yelps is not primarily one of physical pain but one of angry indignation. This is exemplary of the child experiencing a crushing of the false ceiling. As if to say, "Mom, you failed to protect me from my pain," this next layer of collective unconsciousness keeps the false ceiling intact by creating a pipeline of negativity to explain pain. Enter Herr Freud!

Of course, while Freud cracked the golden egg of childhood by his implication that most if not all adult psychic angst originated in the failure of parents to protect their children from pain, the chicken probably came before the egg. The chicken, in this case, was the crumbling lie of pain being avoidable if parents are perfect. With Freud's adroit assistance, humanity got to experience firsthand the birth of this blame-addled collective unconscious archetype.

Though not quite the maven of life's inscrutable ambiguities like his protégée Carl Jung, Sigmund Freud was hardly an intellectual slouch himself. His delineations of consciousness into the realms of ego, id, and superego will benefit us here in our effort to undo the primary mechanism of mental disease. Freud eloquently illuminated how *psychosis,* and its more temperate cousin, *neurosis,* sprung from an innate melee between the wanton impulses of the id and the urbane savoir faire of the superego (with the poor exasperated ego left to futilely mediate). But while Freud nobly pioneered his belief that the priggish Victorian superego of that historical moment was at holy war with the id's sexual audacity, it seems inescapable to me that the core clash is neither purely societal nor strictly carnal in nature.

For the sake of this discussion, I take the liberty to initiate a fourth dimension, at this moment christened *super-id.* Even though the id, as Freud noted, contains one's drives, needs, hungers, and impulses, we will discover that even before it does battle with the superego, it has been tormented with an acquired individualized victimization complex. And so while we have bestowed upon the id the mantle of encompassing the unadulterated animus of our very existence, there is, in fact, a more yawning dominion that lies deeper still. When this cavernous super-id and its primordially dense dukkha envelops an infant with primordial compressive weight, the personal id is already being encoded and predetermined to freak out and attempt to escape this calamitous discomfort.

So, as opposed to idyllically viewing the id as the bastion of human purity, by the time the submarine id attempts to surface, it has already been contaminated with a desperate impulse to explode away from the super-id. As valiant as Freud proved to be in the face of Victorian sexual rigidity, the violence that simmers in the id of humanity (and men especially) is more than a, "Mom, I really want to kill dad so I can have a go in the hay with you" impulse. While sex is indeed convoluted and wrapped like a snake around the rod of human behavior, the desperation at the fundamental core of humanity is an infant's id reaction to super-id's primordial density.

By the time an infant perceives its parents, these 'tall beings' have become beyond proficient in the art of twisting their own pains into the blissful ignorance of guilt, blame and experiential numbness. And so as the very first surge of primordial compression cascades into the baby's physical consciousness, he has no one to learn from as to how to judiciously survive this heavy sensation. When the infant cries, the parents take out their baby books and most often robotically proceed to mistakenly identify what the child is experiencing. We can blame obesity on fast food and instant gratification programming in our present civilization, but parents' cramming breasts and bottles into babies as if their plaintive wails are customarily cries of deprivation, programs the id to believe food is one of the primary solutions to pain.

Worse yet, if the child has been fed and changed and burped and walked around the room and still is crying from the super-id dukkha flooding into its soul, the parents will start to feel their own dukkha activating and beginning to rise in chorus. They will then chase this denseness away, by consciously or unconsciously resenting the baby. Usually this resentment will be sublimated underneath guilt that they are perhaps not being good parents. Though the child will not yet identify his parents' feelings with word thoughts in his little mind, the human foundation for *insult added to injury* is being laid one resentful brick at a time. Dukkha comes into the baby, the baby cries, the parent desperately tries to solve the problem, the Dukkha continues, and the parent feels guilty or irritated (or both) at the child. While 'shaken baby syndrome' is unquestionably at the very far end of this continuum, most if not all parents, though less overt, are still nonetheless extraordinarily upset that the child is not responding well to their baby book promptings.

If on the other hand, we were to know as parents that some of our infant's cries were glorious primal screams, animals howling at the moon and beyond, we could add grace to their existence and not insult. If we were to know as parents that our child's pains were meant to be healed and loved, but not numbed and avoided, we could raise our children to love even the difficulties that life will lay in their paths. If we sat in their bedrooms and meditated on expanding our own soul contractedness so that we might expand our dukkha auras to meet theirs, their ids might stop fearing their super-ids. If we subtracted all the insults and fears we paste upon our infants' pains, we would be turning their potential future mental hells into mental health. And in every way, we should approach these changes with self-forgiveness that we are all still swimming in unchartered waters. I know I sometimes throw out all this information as if it should be easy to change our stupid habits....but dear God I know how hard even the tiniest baby steps away from ignorant bliss are to take.

Chapter 10

Subtracting Insult from Women

While men are regrettably also occasional victims of carnal malfeasance, I intend here to solely examine the particular biosphere of sexual angst swirling through the hearts, minds, and bodies of women. Whether a woman has suffered endless instances of physically undesired hubris from a man or has just had to live in this inexplicable deviant warp, knowing such an interaction is foreseeable, constitutes an oceanic archetypal wound. Unlike other angsts reflected upon in this writing, where subtracting insult from injury eases unnecessary gears of suffering, this collective sexual wound requires a far deeper scope of insight. And it pops my self-possessed balloon to intuit that I possess very little balm in my soul to offer this salient anguish. Still, of course, I am compelled to try.

In the Balkan ethnic cleansings that followed the breakup of Yugoslavia in the 1990s, the ethnicity with the upper hand often systematically raped the women of their enemy. Though it should be supremely patent to rational humans that all female prey of sexual predation are blameless, many of these rape sufferers were ostracized subtly or worse upon returning to their villages. As if their forcefully unlocked female sexuality unconsciously reminded male companions and family members of Adam's sexual fear/hatred of Eve, the women were re-abused by the conjecture that they were even negligibly complicit in their rapes. And though the majority of women will thankfully never directly be victims of rape, enormous psychosexual insults from the same polluted ocean arise trans-personally to burden virtually every female child.

In a more understated but equally charged context, men regularly imagine their lovers eyeing other males and in response, blow up at their paramours with accusations or worse. The archetypal male sexual grief, which I will discuss further on, urges us men on to self-righteously convince ourselves that women's illusory garden of Eden culpability gives us license to hate and blame. For countless women, the amalgamation of male sexually tinged emotional transgressions, are all but as problematic as physical abuse. Not only are the nonphysical 'subtle victims' left with amorphous inner turmoil and less tangible traumas to pin anguish upon, but the well-deserved compassion of loved ones often proves more elusive.

In this psychosexual swamp, *subtracting insult from injury* entails recognizing the classic male fear and resentment of Eve's sexuality at the core of humanity. Your crucial refutation of this biblical curse and the societal mores concerning sexuality that oozes from it likely goes far beyond much of the relatively laid-back tone of transformation otherwise suggested in this book. All of the gradients of borderline personality disorder in women victims of sexual impropriety can be addressed with the following construal: The *allegedly* typical construct of female/male relations that constitutes what sane society considers within the safe parameters of what I call 'the box' is foundationally built on muck and mire. In other words, many women suffering from personality disorders via sexual wounding are being treated as failures by Western culture, which is benumbed enough to accept the box as reality. And unless you have been extremely fortunate enough to find an extraordinary therapist or shaman, the goal of your therapy is sadly too often to steer you back into the cozy, phony confines of the box.

And it is little wonder that perhaps no one intimately cradled your hurt when sexual distortion rained down on your life. In the box, this sexually dysfunctional paradigm is the very fabric of human interaction. We have heard the expression that following a presidential debate, the candidates' handlers 'spin' what has just transpired into whatever drivel they think their half of the sheep will slavishly swallow. Well, in the box, we live in the 'big spin' that men are sturdier and more charismatic, more likely to be the gurus, leaders, writers, and spiritual philosophers. Even the divine feminine often feels as if it is portrayed (albeit subtly) in a slightly lascivious fashion to salve the lust of horny transcendent men.

I'd love to subtract some of your suffering with a spin of my own. Free of the gravity that sucks almost everyone into the box, you are closer to the truth than society's acolytes. Be brave and find those who can support your differences rather than negatively diagnose them. And if this vastly different assessment of your current state of mind/soul/heart is grueling for you to swallow whole, then at the very least, try this. Stop explaining your victimhood to those who fear deep realities beyond their Pollyanna personalities. For if you unwisely share your hurt with the wrong people, you unconsciously reinforce your panic that no one cares. Yes, some people care. And furthermore, in your hypersensitive wounded soul, you can decipher who can care and who, frankly, is just not currently empathetic enough to embrace you.

Subtracting insult from injury might begin then with a fresh light going on in the core of your soul. Oh, that I might ascertain aptitude to offer succor in helping light that candle right now. There is legitimate sanity for your mind/soul/heart to have thrown up its hands in abject defeat. Society has promised us that ordinary life is 'Disneyland good', and sadly, this is a rather large smidgen of a whitish lie. In truth, life is much more like the heroic, daunting trek up your inner Mount Everest. Your experience of sexual hurt and your consequent dissolution of normal numb ego, which constitutes life in the box, has been your trek. You have paid way too many dues, and you are ripe with the probability of some deep healing and ascension of your self-worth.

In the following chapter, I will attempt to identify the fundamental truth from whence all the indignities heaped upon womankind arose. I will try to uncover enough of this depth that we might yet one day soon walk free of the misogyny that engulfs us. I do feel sensitive, though, that you do not take my seeking of objectively culpable forces as in any way diminishing the personal sexual wounds you now feel. If I find a perfect adeptness as I so seek, I will ease some of the objective perplexity surrounding your hurt. If I fall short, please pardon my male limitations.

CHAPTER 11

Patriarchy: The Origin

As health practitioners, we predictably distill much of our hard-earned insight about relieving anguish into our labors with individual bodies and psyches. Replacing this proverbial microscope, though, with a telescope will enable us to broaden our perspective and unravel a tangled web of societal torment as well. To more plainly explain pain and subtract the insults piled upon civilization's past and present-day injuries, I consider it incumbent to systematically deconstruct *why* the divine plan ever begat the patriarchal paradigm. That the odious stench of patriarchy should gain even a grain of propriety through establishing this long-bygone provocation for its creation, I believe, is sadly necessitous. I am convinced there was a primal mandate superseding humanity that mothered the wretched invention of patriarchy. If we can escape our logic's dualistic lens and grasp this, we become empowered to attend to that celestial fiat in a newly evolved way. Many women achingly ponder what in heaven's name ever got into them to have even momentarily acquiesced and subjugated themselves to misogyny in the home, the workplace, and the bedroom. Establishing a model of an objective cosmic motivation for why patriarchy arose, addresses women's poignant entreaty with graciousness and touching realism. And this interpretation will show itself to be infinitely less insulting than some erroneous, injurious implication of women's acquiescence implying their historical indigence of will.

Once upon a foundational time, the cosmic yin and yang conspired *together* to formulate the patriarchal way. As has repeatedly been declared here, the universe before the big bang was encapsulated in a seemingly perpetual imploding dense yin primordial compression. When yang later flung itself into manifestation to explode the density forth with a triumphal blast, life and its inherent joys and tragedies were birthed and bequeathed to us. That the yang boom was able to shatter the primordial compression appears to suggest that this masculinity was greater in power than its yin feminine progenitor. Scientifically, this is excruciatingly far from accurate. Astronomers have ascertained that ninety percent of our cosmos resides in perpetuity in dark matter, and dark energy remnants of the yin primordial compression. This substantiates a profound genuine objective yang debility. The scientific rationale follows that the universe should, by all means, be presently contracting back toward the immensely superior gravity of this yin darkness.

That the universe instead is still expanding is a mystifying, science-defying clue about the patriarchal dominance the yang light and its male human protégées exert. It will be our task to unravel the mystery of this unempirical cosmic expansion and draw insight from its direct correlation to human male power-hogging dominance. Astronomy currently scratches its erudite head as to how the lesser strength of the expanding yang light is prevailing over the preponderant gravity of the yin darkness. With a heaping tablespoon of fable-like anthropomorphosis, I will humbly attempt to fill this void in logic utilizing the following cosmic allegory.

Whatever vivid expansive power the cosmic yang bang had momentarily mustered to divide the sorrow of the primordial yin mother in the, "Let there be light" big bang moment, it was numbingly short-lived. The whole damn thing was about to contract back into the primordial compression before the new universe was spanked on the behind and took its first breath. After the bang, each wave of expanding energy and matter contained a small fraction of the primordial compression, infused with light, the word, cosmic thought, or God's vision. Had the yang expansive force not been a measly ninth as vast as its yin counterpart, but closer to a fifty/fifty balance, the universe might have eventually achieved homeostasis naturally. Then the demonstrative big boy yang light could have spent all of time benevolently serving and thus emancipating the exceedingly dense engrams of primordial yin darkness.

But when the primal yang domain of thought and light correctly perceived the encroaching destiny of the geometrically more prevailing yin gravity of the mother's dark, dense space, the implications were clear. Creation was screwed! Every neuron in every momentarily expanding aspect of the new universe felt the gut punch all at once. Left to its own devices and laws of physics, the post-big bang universe was about to become a monumentally short-lived somebody done somebody wrong song. The primordial compression and her black hole acolytes were morosely setting the table, tucking in their napkins, and preparing themselves for the stars and light almandine feast they were about to re-imbibe. As we know from present-day astronomy, black holes regularly swallow stars whole. Yummy, except this first meal was also foreboded to be the last.

Yang primal thought saw the end was near and astutely concluded, "Screw this." Since the truth was a paralyzing leash that denied the newly expanding cosmos the prospect to journey far and wide, perhaps a monumental white lie might be a superior ticket to ride. The preeminent truth of the yin and her involuting supremacy was buried away in a shielded warped space that would lie at the deepest crevice of the infinite collective unconscious. Replacing the truth, primal thought devised a self-hypnotic conscious story that gave it the reason to believe that *it*, itself, was the big kahuna and that the 'contractive bitch' darkness was an evil afterthought, a jealous creation of a villain named Satan. Let some goody-two-shoes like Buddha or Jesus one day complain about egos and illusions, 'cause for now, man, primal thought was working himself up into a pretty audacious lather.

His white lie of egoistic illusion went something like this: The yang power of light is the greatest power in the universe. Darkness is evil and must be stamped out. Anyone or anything that emanates contractive 'bummer' energy has a massive case of cosmic PMS and must be eradicated. Let the games begin. The me, the I, the self, the man, is the righteous shit that can solve all this dense downer sickness. End of story, morning glory!

With a primal scream that still echoes through the universe, the yang bang thang sang out a victory song that would make Glenn Frey envious and vowed never to look back. In quantum allegiance, every neuron in every morsel of the newly dividing universe joined in the chorus and shouted back in misogynistic harmony, *"Amen, amen."* Mere moments before, the big bang had arisen out of a virtuous perception that the yin density could be lightened through a single explosive shift in the makeup of the cosmos. Suddenly, however, gravitational circumstances tumbling out of control had quickly fomented this anti-darkness megalomaniacal fervor becoming the classic default element of the yang. Countering the cosmic centripetal yin supremacy dragging life perilously inward, primal thought and its mini-me, male neural minions, had evoked a phenomenon of centrifugal power that turned the tide. Alas, patriarchy!

Through holographic neuro-encryption, all of the offspring of the big bang developed a reflective apparatus that magnified and echoed every quantum of inwardly collapsing centripetal energy into an indignant fury of centrifugal reaction. This "and I'll raise you one" reactivity allowed lightweight yang to imbibe and draw on the power of yin, humping it up and outdoing it with its unconscious and conscious chauvinistic last word. The outrage (expanding rage) that yang experienced and expressed whenever yin had the nerve to show her less than dainty, weighty face kept life expanding. Do self-righteous ranting people, hating everything they consider to be "of the darkness" sound at all familiar?

This is the insulting cost of keeping the human ego in its patriarchal-infused blissful ignorance. It needs to turn every pain it experiences into an outward resentful yang thrust. The white lie keeps functioning as long as we continue assuming the sanity of all inward experiences of discomfort being met by a stronger resentful backlash. In a dysgenic waterfall of non-evolving perpetuity, humans became the poster child of this self-deceived cosmic interplay. And Goddess/God could only whisper a muffled prayer that the universe would somehow find incremental healing behind this veil of lies that enshrouds it. And that one day….if only? Meanwhile, in all forms of our popular culture, the forces of darkness speciously are represented as evil. As in American slavery, South African Apartheid, and the holocaust against Native Americans in the New World (just to mention a few), the yang white continually found ways to maintain its superior dint of audacity toward the yin dark. Meanwhile, the power of the idealized, idolized light epitomizes our bogus sense of that which will surmount the 'dark malevolence.' Doctors have always donned white coats and often condescended toward the dark, yucky diseases patients carried forth into their offices. (This awfulness, thankfully, has been amended considerably in the past decade.) Hop-along Cassidy and the other 'good cowboys' always wore white hats, while the 'bad guys' leaned toward darker fashion statements, habitually choosing black hats at their local haberdasheries. We look up at the night sky and fawn over the enchanted light emanating from distant stars, but lest we forget, the darkness is the vast milieu that cradles the little masses of brightness. And yes, who the hell swallows whom? The big, bad black holes with their 90 percent hunger poised to devour stars in the bat of an eye mock the Pollyanna purity of our stargazing innocence. And if they ever felt crossed?

Which brings us to just that. Since the patriarchal yang is such a dastardly cosmic entity, why hasn't the yin sleeping giant awoken? If I were nine times stronger than that which was quelling me, I would quite justifiably pounce and stop the abuse posthaste. And therein lies the rub; I am a man. I, in my embattled male consciousness, generally forgo a higher purpose when I decide I am being damaged or offended. And so it is, this miracle of women with their inherent faith in an ultimate outcome. In the archetypal unconscious of womankind is the memory, the sacrificial magnanimity, bodhisattva altruism, and more to the original subordination.

In the final stages of life's burgeoning, the universal white lie regarding the relative strengths of the sexes was the ultimate calculation of, yes, the female as well as male consciousness. If the pipsqueak, moderately small bang was all the yang could muster, it was not just the tentative, experimental universe that was screwed but She as well. I stated earlier that the yin and yang had conspired together. How profound would the subtraction of insult from yin injury be if we knew that the entire macho patriarchal *his*-story, was a sad product of *her* exigent need for this very indispensable white lie? She acceded to the need for yang to feel bigger than her by making herself smaller—a white lie, I might add, that she determined was the only way she would not be confined for eternity back in her primordial density. In the prototype of all Wizards of Oz, the entire puffed-up power of a male Godhead is false witness atop the female truth at the core of the whole cosmos.

Yin as the primordial involute felt discomfort in her compressing reserve, thus spawning a vibration of agitation.

This rumbling allowed the then-dormant yang to take expression through her, exploding her into innumerable forms. Yang, being less mature or newer to his expression, was bequeathed a sort of Napoleon complex, and yin abided with an ironic Mona Lisa wink. Hark, there is a possible way out of this now, but there apparently was no other way then. A submission of numbered days, the new beginning beckons us. This is *our*-story now—not *his*–story or *miss*-story but our recognized story. With sympathy for the human condition of misapprehensions and the hatred that arises from fear, the future implores us to all be freed from the lie. As such, I humbly, bumbly (but not numbly) offer my personal rendition of the creation myth.

In the beginning, humanity sprang from the double
helix of the Gods in the mirror image of the two
separate cosmic entities, woman housing the procreative
dense yin contractive essence of the Mother, man
the yang explosive movement of the Father.
And just as the Father's hope was predicated on
the exaggeration of his power in comparison to the
Mother, Adam's macho composure depended on his
complete ignorance of Eve's overwhelming dense
needs and the Mother's existence inside her.
Like the other animals of the field, Adam was unconsciously
programmed to 'take' Eve in sexual union on rare occasions.
During these sexual trysts, he entered the thick miasmic core
of the Mother's energy, which Eve carried within her loins.
When his male essence shot into her yin dark matter,
a healing, albeit small, recreation of the big bang
occurred. But so dark and expensive was each *petit*
mort for Adam's fragile yang machismo, that in
between he was programmed to maintain a complete
lack of memory of them having taken place.

Despite the fact that Eve also remained unconscious of the coitus she and Adam occasionally shared, the mysterious tug she experienced during the sexual union predestined her to alter the human species. When early one morning a snake slithering in the grass brushed gracefully against the magnetic warmth of Eve's clitoris, primal woman experienced an epiphany. She was awakened to the forbidden knowledge of her Mother's painful natal essence, throbbing for release within her loins.

The next time Adam came to 'take' her, Eve explained her new awareness to him. Oh that he could but know, as she did, the profound healing that the Mother experienced through their sexual union. Adam ejaculated, looked at Eve as if she were an unpleasant visitor from another planet, rolled over, and fell asleep. But his dreams were newly tortured.

In subsequent times when Adam came for his sexual repast, ingenious Eve attempted assorted means to share with him her fresh, delicate world of sexual awakening. But adamant Adam was resolute in remaining unconscious and resisted her overtures with brutish aplomb.

Eve had one last plan up her sleeve-less birthday suit, and the next time Adam came for carnal feasting, she resisted his less-than-romantic overture. Adam was flummoxed as his innards exploded in spasmodic eruptive hell.

He had little recourse left except to write the first bleeding heart love song and to sue for peace. He took a bite of her aphrodisiacal fruit, and Eve climbed atop him.

They made love often in those heady early days of knowing what the Gods knew, Eve aflame but Adam slowly transforming into a lifeless and gaunt shadow of his former self. For all Adam's bluster, he still was what he was: a small yang essence given the job of healing a dense, powerful darkness nine times his strength.

Growing more and more viscerally aware of this stark
reality did not do wonders for his self-esteem.
The more the Mother's substance inside of Eve found
movement from the primal couple's sexual simulation
of the big bang, the more Adam became emasculated
in the knowledge of her dense singularity.
Finally, the Father jumped into action. At the door between
Adam's conscious mind and the formerly subconscious realm
that Eve had seduced him into, He hung a *'Do Not Enter'* sign.
That 'evil' Eve had seduced Adam into his near demise became
the foundation of the Berlin Wall that would henceforth keep
Adam permanently separated from the subconscious realm
that housed what the Gods knew of the Mother's existence.
Whereas once the only archetypal lie that Adam needed
hanging in the depths of his mind was the one that
stated that men were stronger than women, this second
great lie unequivocally denounced Eve's sexuality.

My particular rendering of the Adam and Eve saga makes it the thirty-three hundred and forty seventh version of how sex gone wrong between great-great-great-great-grandma and grandpa has colored life for the rest of us since the nudist colony in the garden was busted for a ménage-a-trois that included a renowned, well-hung serpent. Not only does Islam have a very analogous tale to the rockin' Judeo-Christian rendition of Eve and that poor sucker Adam, but parallel creation myths are omnipresent as well in diverse cultures throughout the world. And lest we reflexively lean toward vilifying the uptightness of bourgeois Western culture as the sole breast from which this malignant myth has always suckled, let's not forget how the groovy Aztecs sacrificed nubile virgins to their gods. No hip Aztec God worth his macho street cred would deign to take delivery of a forfeit who had spread her hungry legs in Eve-like candor and exposed the black hole of yin domain roiling in her soul. Only virgins dare apply.

As we pour layer upon layer of insult atop the scarcely breathing genuine rawness of our cosmic injury, it is scant wonder that sexuality suffers the greatest obfuscating smokescreen. Our libidinous magma is by far the least straightforward, most explosive, and most mystifyingly embedded aspect of human life. Condense the fluffy puffery of Genesis, and it abridges itself down to Eve commencing a history altering sexual sin resulting in her and hapless Adam having to fig-leaf up their genitals. *Period!* Disobey God, and the punishment is you gotta hide those pesky genitals, *forever*. Don't eat of the tree of knowledge? She *ate*, and they have to cover their genitals. *Sex, sex, sex*. And why is this sex so cloaked underneath trees of knowledge and sin and disobeying God and poor little wimpy Adam being led astray by the slutty Jezebel, Evil Eve? Because, the sexual truth would rip blissful ignorance to shreds. Boom! Because every single act of human sexuality entails the crux of creation's long-daunting, infinite attempt at cosmic homeostasis. Every hobbling, yet thoroughly single-minded, dogged sexual quest, rising from the east of a woman's loins and the west of a man's, holds potential for the phoenix of a new humanity. And the yin/yang facility of two lovers of the same gender is equally as climactic. There is a shrill shriek arcing through light years of space, pounding human sexuality toward establishing a perfect cosmic concoction of the over-pumped yang dynamism breaching the nearly indissoluble wall of yin impenetrability. If and when even a single perfect alchemical moment of yin and yang coitus might ever occur, the blueprint for all future interactions will have been established through quantum entanglement. Until then, the obstinately ambiguous path toward this perfection will endure in its phenomenally formidable arrangement. And as to why the sexual alchemic cosmic moment of hallelujah union has not been, nor will be *easily* reached in the future, we're all dying to know. It is because the magnitude of dukkha that at the outset shall come forth through her penetrated wall will momentarily, at least, swallow the brave yang whole. The French insouciantly designate the male orgasm as a 'small death' (*petite mort*), but frankly, the endgame for the male yang essence is a much more complete fatality than our ignorant bliss can as of yet stomach. And as a male musing over the ultimate terminus of my one-legged Y chromosome, I can only guardedly be hopeful that a charitable Goddess/God has arranged an adequate rebirth if and when I relinquish my full energetic yang template into the vast yin domina.

As a collector of odd puzzle pieces, I add this to our unscrambling mystery. Tiresias is a matchless figure in Greek mythology who attained a preternatural perspective on sexuality. While a young man, Tiresias came upon two snakes entwined in copulation. With his walking staff, he obscenely disengaged the asps, and as reprimand for this transgression against nature, was immediately transformed by the Gods into a woman. Seven years later, moseying in the same forest, Tiresias yet again stumbled upon two snakes awash in sexual bliss. When she once more poked her staff where it didn't belong, becoming again the instrument of reptilian coitus interruptous, she was castigated once again and transmogrified back into a man.

During his/her/his highly erotic time on the planet, Tiresias engaged in vast sexual practice as both a man and a woman. This matchless breadth of genital savvy led the first couple of the Greek pantheon, Zeus and Hera, to call upon Tiresias to resolve a long-standing difference of opinion; "Who," they enjoined, "feels sex more, men or women?" Without a moment's pause, Tiresias explicitly replied that not only did women feel sex more, *they felt it* ***nine*** *times more.* Paradoxically, it was Hera who grew apoplectic at Tiresias's response, and she reacted by striking him blind. Zeus, who had been proven prescient by the "nine times" reply, felt guilty that he had drawn Tiresias into this sightless mess. To make amends, he gave the blinded ambisexual misfit the gift of prophecy. Fittingly, Tiresias later used this consolation prize to foretell the destiny of Oedipus-Rex, the *mother-fucker* who would one day kill his father so that he might gain the opportunity to re-experience the genital supremacy he experienced as an infant in his mother's loins. The Greeks, bless their brazen glimpses at the naked, libidinous ocean of humanity, laid bare with mythological flair fertile pieces of the sexual riddle. I trust you caught the conspicuous detail that astronomers' nine-to-one cosmic ratio of darkness over light was exactly replicated by Tiresias's fastidious estimation of a woman's sexuality vis-a-vis a man's. Tiresias, we can imagine, could have easily approximated ten times as much, but specified *nine*.

And speaking of yin's cosmic preponderance over yang, scientists do not yet know quite how fretful they should be that human male sexual Y chromosomes have been discovered to be severely genetically degenerate. Meaning, that they have lost and continue to be rapidly losing a great percentage of the active genetic material that was present in our ancestors. This, by the way, is not true of the X chromosome, which is doing extremely well, thank you. The X has been shown to retain the essence of all the genetic qualities it had back in samples scientists have gathered from early humanoids. We know that a woman has XX as her sex chromosomes, while a man has XY. Not only then is a man made half out of female chromosomes, but the half of him that makes him male is relentlessly deteriorating over time. I never could quite believe that a huge swath of us males would graciously relinquish the reins of our patriarchy. Well, it looks like it's happening genetically whether we boys like it or not. The patriarchy is hereditarily doomed, and the meek will, thank God and Goddess, inherit the world. Scientific assessment about the Y and its genetic *hari-kari* portends that we boys are losing our chromosomal machismo whether we choose to be cordial or are incapable of such grace. I behold as a man that this change is part of the blessing we all so hungrily crave.

Let's travel back and see what all these sex chromosome shenanigans might be about. Through your virtual reality goggles, you are wayfaring back to the pre-big bang dominion of absolute yin primordial compression. The sisterhood of the X chromosome once was the only inhabitant of this yang-less panorama. At that time, HRH, the Queen's primordial compression, was by her very nature not an inert density but rather an unceasing imploding crusade inward. Every wave of her contractive energy burrowed in ever closer with its sister waves. When one day there was no longer space for inner-directed movement to progress, the first great cosmic rupture transpired. The waves indeed did not initially bang outward but rather tore through each other and shattered their energetic boundaries to open up an 'inner space.' To fit through this tear in the neighboring wave's border, the bigger X waves doffed a leg and morphed into a smaller, sleeker Y design. These disembodied legs, so to speak, were more or less herded into a corral, which occupied space on the yin side of the newly created frontier. While the Ys first truly loved the sensation of free movement in this recently imploded vastness, when they grew tired and felt vulnerable, they reacted as if they didn't have a leg to stand on. These emergent waves then reflexively fled back toward the familiarity and comfort of their dense accustomed gravity and their missing leg. They pulsed with an inimitable urgency that was the earliest DNA for the yang phenomenon soon to be born. Instinctively, the yin universe *knew* that if she resisted the reunion these young yang waves sought with her, their determination would exponentially increase. And this mounting insistence would become the yang crescendo of power that she foresaw could expedite the desired explosion that created light.

As she receded from the yang waves with her "come hither" glance, the Y waves implored with ever-greater demands for reunion. When the importunate pressure of the male waves had reached a sufficiently volcanic climax, the yin universe stopped back-pedaling, stood her ground, and allowed the yang energy to explode back into and through her. And this then was the barely big enough bang.

So, while preceding chapters have demonstrated how the primal white lie and its centrifugal spin of male supremacy account for the way yang maintains an edge over the nine-times strength advantage of the yin, this cosmic propaganda that permeates men's actions and attitudes is just the story of the *visible universe*. In the inner space, unseen dark energy continues to rupture inwardly, sloughing off chunks of herself that are born into single-legged yang waves. These waves persistently seek reunion, which they are denied until their slathers of angry demand have increased their fever-pitch perseverance from within to a tumescent pinnacle. This ensuing aggressive pushing outward toward the receding boundaries of the dense yin world is the second phenomenon keeping the universe expanding. It is this final cosmic truth that I will call the ***illusion*** of the illusion of separation. (The double negative signifying the very real dynamic arising from *separation*.) This parting then completes the story of the origin of male sexuality. And never forget, the nine times as small male Y sexuality has an inferiority complex, not even a one-legged tightrope walker would trade for.

Much of Eastern religion speaks of the illusion of separation, with the inference that our image of egoistic individuality is an illusionary mirage that dedicated meditation can ultimately shatter. All well and good, except that despite the fact that once upon a non-time we *were* all one, the primordial compression needed partition to occur to meet her exigency. We ache to be in 'all is one', and so we try to hypnotize ourselves (and anyone paying us if we are well-regarded gurus) that our separation is merely a silly creation of our egos, "But damn it, Spock, that's just wishful thinking." The illusion of separation is itself an illusion, because indeed the severance is a thoroughly real and preordained phenomenon. The division we experience in the inner world keeps the yang urgency for rejoining, pounding up against the walls of the hidden dark energy. That yang dogged persistent drive toward reunion comes directly up against the yin persistent drive to be released from the hyper-density of the primordial compression. Cosmic alchemy and gradual healing occur at this boundary between these unrelenting and opposing urges, and only this eternal separating and consequent seeking of reunion keep this healing going.

And since women are constructed with powerful yin energy suffusing their ids, their egoistic sense of separation from the primal yin mother is comparatively slight compared to men's. Their sexual will is primarily concerned with the intricate alchemic dance involved in bringing men toward them at a nearly impossible speed and intensity to maneuver. The ids of we men, conversely, are generally flooded with yang segments of sloughed-off density, which are cosmically programmed to agonize with separation and urgently thrust outward back toward oneness. Between this insistence throbbing in our male ids and the primal white lie blaring in the archetypal male unconscious, our fucked-up macho behavior is tragically preordained and predictable. But every long journey begins with a first step, and I am significantly more than a bit optimistic that within this hypothesis is ample grist for the mill of poignant transformation. Some of the specifics for formulating a therapeutic technique around this premise is work I have not entirely completed. There are, however, palpable road signs available that could be employed in the transmutation of male sexual ignorant bliss. First, we must face the hurtful truth that we men are harming women with some aspects of our maleness. Then we can be liberated to gain the sovereignty to reinvent yang alchemic propensities.

Until then, the broken wing of our inter-sexual alchemy

relies on every wedding providing conjugal blinders. Thus do Mr. and Mrs. "take this man and take this woman" block out the divorce lawyers lurking in a rear pew of the church silently mouthing "ka-ching" as the newly betrothed join the inevitable queue toward married sexual downfall. But if we can bear the prospect that carnal malfunction is objectively the default destination of most romantic relationships, rather than a series of hundreds of millions of, "Darn, if only that hadn't have happened" personal breakdowns, we can finally grab the bull by its horny horns. We can then pass from the ignorant bliss of the wedding day, through the "truth hurts" phase in which relationships suck, and enter the "truth will set us free" chance to work on the enigmatic puzzle objectively, without bias and blame. Subjective pointy-fingered explanations for relational angst are 100 percent destined for disappointment. Conversely, a universal understanding of the breakdown provides new avenues down which struggling couples might walk hand in hand. Through recognition of the unresolved species-wide yin/yang interplay at the core of all human relations, we could establish a base camp from which to climb and hopefully ultimately overcome the mountain of male/female disunion crippling us.

While far more labyrinthine than this, for the sake of intellectual luxury, let's once again make a sweeping statement that women house yin and men house yang. While the seen universe stretches outward for billions of light-years, the unseen, inside-out realm in point of fact holds nine times as much cosmic substance, as well as the key to universal hope. In this inner alternate universe, the primal design is continually birthed. Heavy yin particles slough off one of their legs, becoming yang. Yang particles continue pressing out of the inner realm, against the yin partition, and eventually burst out into the seen universe. Our human ids, unconscious realms, dreams, and souls are directly linked to this inner yin domain of dark matter and dark energy and its brilliant wo-manipulation creation of yang.

Extrapolating how this yin/yang interplay is embodied by women and men, just might afford us the slightest advantage in addressing the human war of the sexes.

By cosmically maintaining the mantle of *no*, the yin female accomplishes the following: she holds the yang back from too soon dissipating itself and becoming once again yin itself. Also, by denying the yang easy entrance back into the primordial compression, she frustrates the yang into eventually building up a head of steam and crashing through her resistance and thus big-banging life into this outer yang world. A human woman personifies this *no* through her seeming outward attitude toward sexuality. An example is this: a woman wears a revealing blouse, and when she sees a man staring at her cleavage, she often reflexively moves her hands to conceal the sex. At the same time, the woman cosmically is id-driven to wear the sexy top because she in due course needs yang energy to pierce through her 'no' barrier. This in no way means a female is a conscious tease or any of the human put-downs that men might ascribe to women.

The one-legged yang Y sex chromosome wears the mantle of, "Yes, I gotta have it." Until it breaks back into and through the yin domain, it is always ready for the change, continuously feeling both frustrated and incomplete. The caricature of the horny man at all times ready to have sex, and willing to do it with any number of random women, is this cosmic expression of the male *yangst* (yang angst). Yes, the incomplete degenerative Y lurks in the male soul, desperate to regain the footing lost in its cosmic amputation. In the ugliness of rape lies not only the patriarchal persona of male expectancy and alleged superiority, but the Y's kamikaze reaction to its crippled destiny. The Y, as its approaching genetic obsolescence proves, is an impermanent manifestation. If and when it breaks through the female *no* and gains purchase, it will feel at least momentarily the ecstasy of wholeness. That male attitude that women possess something that belongs to us is cosmically betrothed to reality. It is a crazy, fractured, oft-tragic actuality, but it is reality. After the *ignorant bliss* of Valentine's Day flowers, the *truth hurts* mountain to climb here is daunting. All this thoroughly screwed-up crap between men and women *is based on cosmic reality.* This truth that hurts is the beating heart of an understatement.

As to the rock and the hard place cosmic conundrums sexually facing the X factor in our equation, let me forlornly count the ways. If a woman relents too quickly to a Y's need to reacquire his missing leg, the shortsighted climax brings celestial woe. A human male routinely loses sexual interest in a woman he has long sought as soon as she has uncrossed her X and let him enter her inner wall. This is because if his inertia of need/motion is too dawdling, he will gain back his missing leg, attain completion, be transformed back into an X himself, fail to burst through her outer wall, and run. He indeed felt a profound lacking as a one-legged Y, but as a two-legged X, he has become a she. And the inertia of rest that she, the X, holds in a heavy, dense vault, invites male flight. She longs to hold him there so he might one day burst the outer wall of her density and help create a yin/yang world of space and time. But in being held there, he loses his yang incompleteness, his reason for moving, his edge, and his bravura. He adds insult to her injury by believing she lacks some sexiness that would give him more emotive passion and inertia of motion.

If we men and women can even remotely begin to view each other objectively, like pieces of a puzzle that infinite consciousness has not yet completed, we might approach our alchemic sexual and romantic mission with tender trepidation. As I have reiterated throughout this book, we who work diligently to slough our yucky egos would be wise to admit the dualism we still sadly employ at the core of our romances. If my tale is true, as I wholly sense might be so, the cup has **never** been full. The illusion that romance should be perfect and once was so only fosters the resentment for each other when we sense the true emptiness of the cup.

Chapter 12

Astronomy, Buddha, and Dukkha

When one of my children came home from a college lecture and conveyed astronomy's principal theory of that which existed prior to the big bang, it set my inquisitiveness aflame. "All the energy and matter presently inhabiting our entire expanding universe," she imparted, "was originally squeezed into a tiny black hole-like singularity known as the *Primordial Compression*." Years ago, I learned one of the essential laws of physics is that every action has an equal and opposite reaction. Primal imploding compression therefore equally and oppositely consummating in a big bang explosion made unimpeachable sense. Furthermore, a cosmic rationality emerged, that the moment the Bible trumpets, "And God said let there be light," is the same as the big bang. If all that existed pre-bang was quintessentially dense, dark, compressed, and dare I say, experientially in pain, an altruistic God would absolutely beneficently pull off an outrageous, emancipating "let there be light" moment.....wouldn't He?

And if everything since is comprised of one of the imploding segments of that primordial dark compression, now partnered with an infusion of the pain-relieving expanding yang light propellant, a utopian vision of cosmic recovery emerges. Trusting that God didn't create humans and one day capriciously decide how groovy it would be for us all to suffer endlessly, a 'cup half full' grasp of our agonies offers itself. I embrace this great Goddess/God whose only recourse upon facing the challenge of the primordial compression was to explode it into billions of neurologically bioactive entities. Instead of one huge cosmic embryonic agony, there would be innumerable, throbbing, sentient "God-lets," each imbibing the nectar of the ever-effulgent heart of God. So the bangin' "let there be light" hoedown has been a hallowed success. Instead of a singular black hole-like universe, objectively experiencing eternal anguish, we have our cosmos being healed by each of us, one survivable, albeit subjective, hurt at a time. And some fine day, which I sense is ever so much more rapidly approaching than we can fathom, the epic marathon of the human race will beyond doubt be entirely run. One unbelievably auspicious moment, the veil will be lifted off God's universal truth, and we will know that every sorrowful last drop of pain experienced on this planet arose to be healed by our humanity and reaped by the Goddess. And in her reaping, she has accumulated so many emulsified engrams of the former angst that the beauty of her work and ours will fill our hearts with redemption and forgiveness for every sad moment of history. Yes, humanity has paid the dues, and we will not end in some apocalyptic agony (we have, quite frankly, had our agony already, thank you).

Though I refer to myself facetiously as a semi-Buddhist (having proven myself a poor excuse for a full-fledged devotee of the Buddha), my life has been made more euphoric through the grace of a few glorious Buddhist teachers. Meanwhile, I also have discovered that no religion is so fraught with all the contesting implications of a single defining utterance, as is Buddhism by its seminal term, *dukkha*. Unsurprisingly then, it was during a lecture about this gravid unit of language that a cloud-busting new channel was permanently carved in my mind. For those unfamiliar with Buddhism and its Four Noble Truths, some backstory here is befitting. There is a tale (which not all Buddhists see eye-to-eye on) about the aftermath of Buddha's Enlightenment. When his fellow mystical seekers awoke one morning and beheld the transformation that had transpired with Siddhartha Gautama, they cajoled him to expound upon how he had found his way to this exalted state of nirvana. To their abject shock, Buddha was anything but spontaneously forthcoming. In response to his reticence, they essentially articulated the twenty-five hundred–year-old version of, "Dude, I thought we were all in this together." As he gazed at the wasteland of their desperate egos, the portentous shilly-shallying of Buddha's reluctance bespoke the aptness of his discretion most eloquently.

A majority of us in the West know only the most cursory new-age ballyhoo about Buddhism. Om, incense, and other Buddhism light (Bud light) inanities generally fulfill all the deliberation we expend on this and other Eastern religions. But for those who have beheld the nearly scandalous connotations attached to Buddha's discourse on *dukkha*, the food for thought can stretch into a banquet. When Buddha wisely deduced that the elucidation of his enlightenment was not going to be so easily digestible, he had all too well discerned the second holy cliché—the truth hurts. Jump on a search engine and type in *Buddhism* and *pessimism*. Then prepare for a long spell poring over an avalanche of vehement criticisms that Buddha's first noble truth about *dukkha* was a pessimistic, blasphemous view of life. In reaction and drenched in apologia, devout Buddhists accordingly too often feel obliged to sugarcoat Buddha's fearless declaration.

In retrospect, it is patently clear why Buddha responded with trepidation to his compatriots' ardent desire to learn how he had reached an enlightened state. Buddha's emergence into a nascent ability to behold a complicated truth about humanity is the antithesis of the pabulum normal egos demand. When Buddha finally relented, agreeing to share how he had attained his nirvana–like state, he did so with an unwavering proviso: "I will teach you, but only if you follow my journey of inner awakening in the exact order that I convey it to you." He thus laid out his cosmic curriculum beginning with the Four Noble Truths and ending in the Noble Eightfold Path. Buddha beheld that it would be an inauspicious task to take these new disciples down the paradoxical *endarkened* road to enlightenment. They would want to jump to the last step, but Buddha knew the real hurdle would be getting them to take the daunting first step. Embrace *dukkha*. But what then is *dukkha*?

Buddhists alternately describe *dukkha* as suffering, disappointment, anxiety, disillusionment due to attachment, stress, or a host of other abhorrent-sounding feelings. Buddha is said to have proclaimed, "I have taught one thing and one thing only: *dukkha* and its cessation." Understanding what *dukkha* is, then, would seem to be as important for a Buddhist as a Christian having a real clue as to why Christ died on the cross. (More about that later.) If we interchange the word *healing* in place of *cessation*, we are about to advance a huge part of the journey as to how to subtract insult from injury. During a discourse I attended, a Buddhist teacher proclaimed that the word *dukkha* arose from two Sanskrit words, *du* and *akkha*. These two words roughly translated to "dense space." I was dumbstruck.

Astronomy moment: primordial compression Buddhist moment: dense space

Boom, that sure sounded like the same darn thing to me.

Like a trans-generational game of *telephone*, the fact that Buddha's wisdom about dukkha got sullied as it passed down through the varied resistances it encountered, is woeful but plausible. Alas, human minds look for predictable, palatable, victim-hued human feelings to describe Buddha's indescribable instinct that everyone was experiencing the primordial compression. So, defining *dukkha* as presumably avoidable suffering is a typically human, ignorantly blissful interpretation.

The abbot of a nearby Buddhist monastery once proclaimed that all the hullabaloo about dukkha could be condensed down into the following sentences: Every human will experience dukkha, but if we allow ourselves to experience it as if it will soon pass like a lousy day of weather, it will just be pain. If we experience dukkha as if it has personally victimized us, it becomes our suffering. If we one day understood that dukkha is coming through us, not happening to us, we could 100 percent cease the practice of adding insults to our injuries. Ultimately, there can be no compromise here. *You are not your story*. You cannot have it both ways. You are not in full spiritual bloom, while concurrently running your dualistic victimization myths about why *you* have pain. Even we ardent spiritual seekers are unfortunately inclined to use transcendent language to describe everything ***except*** our pains. C'mon, this is endgame! It is time to homogenize our perceived personal sufferings into a larger cosmic perspective.

While Buddha showed us that dukkha happens to us all, karma is quite another phenomenon. Karma is each individual's personal amalgam of the dukkha one has already healed (good karma) and the dukkha one is chasing away through resentments (bad karma). When dukkha is *sent* to you to heal, and you *re-sent* it away with your resentment in a return-to-sender envelope to God, the cosmos will one-up your resistance with a bad karma package of hurt you surely will regret. If you want only good karma in your life, there is a direct way to achieve this. Do not resent the painful challenges that come your way, and do not wait for your allotted dukkha to catch up with you and perhaps take you by surprise. Instead, develop a meditation practice in which you sit intimately with dukkha and let it weep and sweep through you. Birth this beloved need of Goddess/God through your heart's mercy, and you will never require bad karma again.

Chapter 13

Jesus: The Final Hours

I have previously pigeonholed myself a semi-Buddhist and with tongue correspondingly planted in the opposite cheek, I likewise decree myself barely a semi-Christian. Yet since some of Christ's apostles so audaciously chickened out on him, then turned around and helped write their justification-drenched "covering their own ass" version of events, *the Bible,* I believe I warrant a say as well. I trust the iconoclastic Rabbi Jesus won't mind if an ex-Jew nonconformist like me takes a shot at conjecturing the core message *The Cross* conferred upon us.

I'm going to say it for you: I have a busload of hubris. Here I am, implying not only that the dark underbelly of Buddha's teaching has been predominantly camouflaged but also that Christ's crucifixion has, by the same token, been similarly cloaked. So many Christians, alas, aspire to get to the mountaintop by way of a helicopter rather than a life-altering climb. They, like most adherents of most religions, have turned the darkness unearthed by Christ into vanilla Simon Says exercises. Simon says, "Read that section of the Bible, or chant those words ..." and abracadabra, the gruesome visage of Christ's abject torture gets a fetching facelift, and you get to feel a religious hard-on about yourself.

Cutting to the chase, the aforementioned disciples turned

their wetting-their-pants denial of their Savior into the ultra-convenient mantra, "He died for our sins." Look, if only dying had been the quid pro quo Christ was required to pay for our sins, he could have laid down on a sword and been gone in ninety seconds. If God's favorite child could have just died promptly and not had to suffer unspeakable pain, wouldn't you surmise God might bypass the necessity for the multiple hours of agony? But we buy it hook, line, and sinker when the apostates cheerily assure us, "I wuss out at the critical moment of my dear Jesus's thorny coronation, and rather than paying this little detail much ado, I declare that my chicken-heartedness didn't damage anything. What's the problem? *He died for our sins."* Let's get this straight: he undergoes unspeakable agony (at least Mel Gibson's *Passion of the Christ nailed* that part), and I tuck my little tail into my groovy disciple's robe, slink away with a hot future best-selling book idea, and voila, everything's cool. Apostate doesn't sound too far removed from apostle; it can't have been too big a betrayal.

"I'm sure relieved we didn't have to go the Savior's '*follow me, I am the way*' route. Ouch, those nails in the hands alone were enough to convince me instead to accept the disciples' whitewashed version of things." But what if? What if God had his only begotten Son go through this horrendous physical, soul-shattering experience because he felt agonizingly compelled to give the rest of us a blatantly unsubtle tip-off about pain? The lesson of the cross isn't Christ's willingness to die, nor is it Christ's rebirth into eternal life. Christ agreed to sacrifice himself *before* the crucifixion, and he arose *after* the crucifixion. Our absolute brain freeze about what occurred *during* his time on the cross is the most obstinate, mind-blowing ignorant bliss imaginable. We are only able to remain a species wholly ignorant about why God created us with such a vast capacity to suffer pain because we allow ourselves the fuzziness of mind to fail to catch why God had his favorite child go through the entire measure of his agony.

And even with all his prior willingness, the pain was so great that even Jesus temporarily could not fathom how his Father would have him suffer so greatly. "Father, why have thou forsaken me?" Remember, these words were cried out mere minutes before Jesus healed his entire allotted dukkha, reached enlightenment, and passed from his body with spiritual completion. Jesus repeatedly had pledged that he would love God with all his heart and mind. He was thus recruited to be *the one.* He was assigned to show all of God's dysfunctional children that they must rectify their resentment and slavish adherence to the programmed numbness that led them to harm others rather than experiencing pain themselves. And speaking of disobedience, for my money there is no Satan or Devil. Evil, in all its hideous formations, arises incrementally through our stated programmed avoidance of pain. Since our innate archetypal memory recalls that our purpose on the planet is to bring darkness up from the gut/soul to be healed, and we counter that subterranean instinct through the ignorant logic of our egos, something's gotta give. What gives is, instead of mining dukkha out of our own souls, we mine it out of others. And just like we mine our dear Mother Earth with a wanton disregard, we perpetrate violence on our sisters and brothers. By convincing ourselves that another needs the pain we are causing them (physically or emotionally), we satisfy the primal drive in us to bring dukkha forth. And so, evil is this avoidance of bravely bringing our own dukkha up to be healed, while forcing the dukkha forth from our enemy.

As to the lesson of the cross, what golden nugget was gifted to us through Christ's wrangling with his Father before regaining faith in the final moments? And what did our all-knowing God expect would be the outcome of this close call? Was Jesus's temporary feeling of abandonment preordained or not? And what resounding truth did God ultimately share with his Son that assuaged the boy's doubt and set him free to finish his appointed holy mission? It is certainly counterintuitive that any father would entreat his most beloved child to suffer so greatly, unless ...

Assuming that God's petition to Jesus was a desperate measure, why was God so at the end of his tether? Why force Jesus to agonize so grievously that the beloved Son nearly failed? On Passover night, the Christ beseeched his Father to find a less-drastic way to drive home the point (painful pun intended). But God did not, or *could not,* relent. There will be no softer line, for God is desperate. Have we ever considered why? In older times, God spared Abraham's boy at the last moment. Did God, in acknowledgment of his Son's absolute fidelity, consider testing Jesus's faith and likewise, at the end of the day commuting the death sentence?

While the crucifixion was unfolding in real, tormented, and anguished time, and the disciples indeed were astonishingly denying Jesus, was *even God* taken back a wee bit? I mean if even some of the twelve closest to Christ chose the cozy fecklessness of cowardice, what could God's plan to use Jesus's martyrdom to inspire sacrifice in others have looked like at that moment? Might this have even taken the wind out of God's sails long enough to mitigate *even his faith* in the crucifixion experiment? With diarrhea running down the Savior's legs, amalgamating with blood, urine, tears, bile, and vomit, and with bugs crawling into every crevice of his darling body, might Jesus have noticed that God had suddenly grown rather oppressively hushed? Was this the moment of Christ's doubt? Was the entire situation spiraling out of control in wretched probability of going so far awry that all of Jesus's anguish, perchance, would be for naught?

And if we are psychically courageous enough, let's consider that whatever success was gleaned from the crucifixion was, in the end, a far closer call than we ever imagined. This was not a beneficent God slam-dunk. We know Jesus had his moment of questioning; might God also have? Can we imagine them both having to scramble and think on their feet? (Ah, the bad puns.) "Ahem, God! I'm still up here. Where in the heck are you? Are you having doubts? Well, it's a little too late for that, at least as far as I'm concerned. I thought you had this in the bag. Yes, of course, my hands hurt."

And, as long as I am way out on a limb, squarely in the blasphemous demolishing of sacred cows business, let's try this one out. Only Judas, having obeyed Jesus's command to have the Romans delivered, was willing to follow his Master. Judas, as opposed to the others, took his own life. Maybe he embodied Christ's "follow me; I am the way" stuff more seriously than the deniers. Maybe the cowardly disciples, when not auditioning for the part of the lion in The *Wizard of Oz,* made efforts to tarnish Judas's deeds to exonerate themselves. I don't know—just a hunch.

Chapter 14

The Sun

From the archaic German word *Sunna,* the goddess in Germanic paganism, our sun has a critical moral to demonstrate regarding our societal enterprise to *Subtract Insult from Injury*. While this ancient German civilization was more perceptive to a crucial Goddess-like aspect of the sun, modern culture generally regards the sun in a linguistically male way. The moon conversely, which reflects the supposedly dominant male sun, is thus beheld as female .

We conceptualize our nearby life-giving star through this masculine template because true to form, we identify the radiating yang power of the sun as its essential attribute. We require and adore the heat, light, and photosynthesis it openhandedly affords *us*. We rarely, if ever, stop to imagine what she, Sunna, is experiencing. The nuclear fusion in her core is the embodiment of sacrificial servitude at its most quintessential. While her labor pains and contractions never end, weaning us from her warm breast is hardly an option. If she ever got sick of creating the fiery eternal damn-fire burning in her core, our goose would be cooked ... or frozen. We've heard the aphorism *love hurts;* well, this life-sustaining love hurts in the core of the sun, eternally. And while our first reaction might be to pooh-pooh this whole line of thought, we do so at the risk of being like the infant who scoffs at taking an interest in the mother from whom it is suckling.

We have heard it said that some people have 'sunny' dispositions or 'warm' personalities. We have been told that passionate, dedicated people have the fire in their belly to reach their goals. We have listened to fiery orators and felt sunlight bursting from the souls of certain charismatic people. Conversely, we have heard some troubling people described as 'radioactive.' In short, it is evident that humans are created from all the cosmic forces that are at play in the field of dark and light. Just as the sun burns fiercely in the core of her darkness and bequeaths us warmth and light from her devoted pursuit, so do we humans precisely follow this prototype.

Miscellanies of the primordial compression presently stored in black holes, dark matter, and dark energy are emitted via our super-ids, enter our core/soul, and in quantum strategy are there converted into matter and energy. Within mitochondria in each of the hundreds of billions of human cells, this conversion creates calories of heat, the literal fire in the belly to live. And then, akin to mini-suns, the fire built up in the core is transmitted toward the outskirts. There on the periphery, it becomes our actions and art, our love, our service, our sunshine, our energetic capacity to accomplish our visions and dreams, and the heat of our passions.

Now that you understand the fiery pain alchemized inside you in every moment, you will forgive yourself that some days it seems you are being devoured by fire. You are. Stop insulting yourself that you are not always in a good mood. Stop labeling yourself with negative psycho-babble monikers when you are, like the sun, merely a servant of the cosmic plan. It's not Mercury in retrograde; it's your hallowed primal service.

Of the trillions of cells that constitute your physical presence, life astonishingly replenishes itself with fifty to seventy billion new ones every twenty-four hours. Fifty billion little bundles of joy daily join the menagerie of life that you mentally try to cram into your ostensibly single, particular egoistic self. As to the relatively old codger cells being asked to make way and give up their assignments, apoptosis, programmed cell suicide, has that all covered. While *suicide* is ordinarily a tragically negative word in our semantic landscape, picturing all the perky new cellular beings lining up to assume their roles in the somatic universe of your body, mitigates the linguistic sting.

Apoptosis, as opposed to necrotic death of cells due to disease or physical trauma, is part of the natural cellular process of death and rebirth. When a mitochondrion senses that its ability to manufacture energy for cellular functions is ebbing, it sends out a signal that its demise would be a wise move for the good of the whole. Apoptotic processes respond to the signal, and a mercy killing of the tiny bugger is accomplished. And billions of times a day, phagocytic hungry white blood cells gobble up the exploded debris of the dearly departed. Their replacements, the preschoolers, report for duty, hat in hand.

C'mon, admit it—did death ever sound so delightful before? If the darned thing didn't hurt, it would be just an awesome riot. Yup, that little detail, *pain*. Death (and rebirth as well for that matter) hurts. Every day fifty to seventy billion little deaths (very petit morts) are burning through our nervous systems like a gentle brush fire sweeping over the landscape. And fascinatingly, we humans have found the way to suppress much of this nagging, gnawing pain of apoptosis. In fact, if we exhibit too much abundant success in this clampdown on dying, we beget *cancer*. The number one feature of cancer is that its metastatic relentless hunger *defies* apoptosis. Cancer cells are equipped with mechanisms that *deny* death. That's why cancer is so hard to beat back sometimes. We are so impatient with pain and death that we have created our own little biological mutation, and it is cancer. Cancer cells throw up their little hands and say, "Why do you hate us? We're only doing what you wanted. You hate death, and so we have manifested to reflect your desire."

And while we are delving into areas of concrete science, perhaps you have seen the visage of the ALS-ravaged, dazzling astrophysicist Stephen Hawking and remained unaware of his groundbreaking research into black holes. For over thirty years, science followed Hawking's lead, accepting his premise that absolutely no light escapes once it is swallowed by a black hole. Then, about a decade ago, Hawking appeared at a significant scientific symposium and startled those in attendance by stating that he had been wrong all those years. Evidence now pointed to a new reality that some light was, indeed, emitted after having been ingested by a black hole.

I am here to tell you that Hawking was right *both* times. Impossible? Listen! In the thirty years since Hawking's first appraisal of light's suicidal relationship with darkness (black holes), a monumental shift occurred in the relationship of the two primal forces. Now I know that what I am about to share may utterly stretch the limits of your submission to the unimaginable, but if you've read this far, maybe you are ready to embrace what is nearly beyond belief. Thirty years ago, the light of our conscious minds was mostly oblivious to objective darkness. Then something happened. Ever-increasing numbers of our species began to look upon what they initially referred to as each individual's 'shadow side.' Whereas thirty years ago, we beheld darkness purely in an adverse context, recently more of us began to examine our resistance to the light-less domain.

This emergent acceptance to feel the shadow from whence Dark matter and energy arises, began transforming cosmic light into a force willing to be swallowed and emulsified by the primordial compression. Fittingly, scientists have christened the energy emerging out of black holes as Hawking's radiation. Every brave moment we refrain from resentment and embrace our dukkha, we create Hawking's radiation and fulfill our cosmic mandate/womandate.

Chapter 15

Quantum Physics

Perchance, if there is but one thing you have been exposed to pertaining to quantum physics, it is *the double-slit experiment.* About a hundred years ago, iconic experimentation unintentionally revealed that when electrons were fired at a photosensitive plate behind a metal barrier with two slits in it, the electrons sometimes behaved like particles of matter and other times whimsically comported themselves as waves of energy. The inadvertently discovered determining factor behind the bizarrely fickle behavior of these particles/waves was the act of observation itself. When an apparatus was arranged to observe the electrons going through the slits, they ventured through the photographic plate as particles. When the device was turned off, the same electrons quixotically scurried through the photographic plate as energy waves. Some classical Newtonian physicists, who had spent lifetimes establishing concrete objective scientific laws, found this indecision on the part of these wave/particles to be downright unnerving. It was one thing to wax poetic and ascribe beauty as being in the eyes of the beholder. But for the eyes of the beholder to be the pivotal influence behind electrons acquitting themselves like matter one time and energy waves the next, was beyond the pale.

The quantum law ascertained from this experiment was that

the act of observation collapses energy waves into particles. In other words, a reality has never been as concretely real as we pay scientists to prove it is. Just the opposite! That the eyes (perceptions) of the beholder determine how and when quanta of energy give up their free lifestyle and put on a proper suit of clothes makes us humans the moment-by-moment architects of the visible universe. That suit of clothes gives a formerly naked, limitless quantum of energy shape, substance, identity, and visibility. So while we humans blithely assume that most of our thoughts are little more than Facebook and Twitter fodder, our mental machinations quite literally emit enthusiastic enzymes that narrate to energy waves what they shall become. Our thoughts not only write the story of our lives but create all the scenery to flesh out these variegated fairytales to boot.

Another phenomenon associated with the double-slit experiment was this: when one of the slits was blocked off, the electrons being fired at the photographic plate always behaved like particles. So while the act of observation mentioned above was proven to collapse waves of energy into particles of matter, lack of options did as well. The similarity between the single slit and a singular point of view seems to be the common ground behind electrons choosing to be matter rather than energy waves. In other words, when there is a single slit, there is a single predetermined path for the electrons, and when there is observation or point-of-view, there is also predetermination. The expectation, to see or measure something, connotes predetermination. On the other hand, when waves are given a choice, they choose *both*. If given a thousand choices, they would ruminate quite maturely and then choose all thousand slits.

What downright caught in Albert Einstein's craw about quantum physics culminated years later when the theory of quantum entanglement made the role of the observer even more influential than the double slit had. What entanglement demonstrated was that two particles that have ever been conjoined, will remain entangled forever, even if they become separated by astronomical distances. So, if an observer pinpoints the electrical polarity of a particle as having a positive charge, its one-time twin particle will simultaneously gain a negative charge even if it is trillions of miles away. Poor Einstein was apoplectic and called this "spooky action at a distance." He went to his grave angrily unconvinced that the observer not only collapsed an energy wave into the observable positive charge mentioned above but that the information was then communicated faster than the speed of light, forcing the twin particle to assume the opposite charge.

As brilliant as he was, Einstein's obsession to discover and establish inflexible material laws that would regulate the universe, is at the heart of how we humans erroneously define our experiences. Such is the nature of human discernment that we ache to conquer the ambiguities of the universe through our perceptual ability to categorize everything. Our insatiable acquisition of knowledge dovetails with our belief that we humans are the lion-tamers that shall bend the wild universe to our intellectual will. Any teenage energy wave that isn't discerning enough to pick the best of the thousand slits needs a patriarchal thought form to reign it in. But the fact that our function as observers keeps determining moment by moment how matter and energy behave makes a conquerable, comprehensible universe keep squirming just beyond our slippery, opinionated grasp.

There is but one last aspect of quantum mechanics to explore before we hazard to subtract insult through these subatomic frameworks. While every wave of energy and every particle of matter dualistically contain the capacity to transform into the other, like water and ice, they also behave quite distinctly from one another. When the original electron fired at the double slit shocked scientists, it was because of the following quantum property of energy known as *probability waves*. In other words, before an energy wave is collapsed into matter, it consists of an infinite amount of possible and probable outcomes for its journey. Indeed, before the observer collapses the possibilities into the single particle beheld by 'point of view,' energy behaves riotously and uncontrollably, as it did in its days before the big bang. Back then, over-compressed waves of energy were restless to go anywhere or do anything to break away from the imploding anguish of their existence.

So while our minds unconsciously perceive an energy wave with the implicit desire to collapse it into a definable little entity, the wave rolls its eyes at us, snickers at our simple-mindedness, and occasionally relents. When free, though, to choose as in the double-slit experiment, the particle, unencumbered by the magnetism of hungry human cerebral expectation, will frolic into its wave-form, which blithely decides to travel through both slits. Releasing waves of energy from the presumption that they should squeeze themselves into human thought forms is to liberate Goddess/God. When Einstein's petulance about the possibility/probability aspect of the quantum world resulted in his notorious quote, "God doesn't throw dice," renowned quantum physicist Niels Bohr countered, "Stop telling God what to do." Indeed, if we could mitigate our cosmic hubris, we could alter the concept of 'mind over matter' into an innovative model of 'mind into matter.' As the quantum world has established our role of the beholder in the emergence of matter from energy, we humans could humbly learn to perceive the monumental responsibility inherent in such a truth.

And so, the simplest way to imagine *subtracting insult from injury* through quantum truth is to imagine a relay race. You can either choose to participate in the race, or you can sit in the stands, bellyache about your pains, and cheer and jeer those you perceive to be running in your stead. Everything that exists (matter and energy) has been proven to have been created with the express quality of being eternally ready to be manifest in innumerable ways. And of itself, it has minimal prejudice as to where or how it will be manifest. Instead, it waits to be perceived, and only through observation does it individuate out of the field of energy that has traveled forth ever since the big bang. While the first runner in the relay race was the dual yin and yang aspects of God, this cosmic couple made us in their own image to carry on the task. While particles and waves behave according to quantum laws, part of the vast mystery of life is that these interchangeable units are only birthed into our known cosmos through the electromagnetic force of a human thought/feeling. Like Monday-morning quarterbacks, we have until now often tended to look backward at life. We react to it as if, 'like the tide' it semi-regularly is striking up against us, and only after meeting us awaiting our editorial opinions.

But if we instead ran forward in the relay race, with the wind of the cosmic field at our backs, we could co-create the best of the possibility/probability outcomes that pre-manifest particle/waves could become. If you can imagine your soul-being as now having just a single slit, we can imagine what it might take to add at least a second slit, which would let the cosmic field come to you as waves of energetic possibilities. What presently makes you a single-slit kind of guy or gal is your ego with its singular expectations, demands, issues, stresses, attitudes, particular pointy points of view, and overall sense of 'deserving.' This egoistic belief is that you deserve things to go well, and if they don't, they will be filed in the "return to sender" place in our souls we call *re-sent-ment*. So you have a single slit that awaits life's proper treatment, but if you experience something rough, you reserve the right to re-send it back to destiny with an "I'm peeved, just why have you forsaken me God" sticky note attached. While twenty-first-century pop culture encourages you to believe that holding oneself as a deserving person is healthy, let's explore that word more acutely. When you *de*volve or *de*stroy or *de*construct or *de*tach or *de*mand or *de*lay or *de*base or *de*fy or *de*grade, the *de* prefix is pretty obviously *de*leterious. And so if quantum life and its cosmic field await each of us to serve it, but we wait behind our *de*serving single-slotted ego to be served by Daddy God ourselves, the conundrum is clear. Our "insults added to injury"-laden story that we present to others and use to swathe ourselves in the baby blanket of self-pity is birthed of such disenchanted *de*serving.

So let's try a quantum experiment using our heart and soul as double slits to replace the single slit that is our egoistic mind. The tide is coming in, and the cosmic wave still expanding out from the big bang with its quantum multiplicity of perceivable potential manifestations is about to enter us. This surging ripple of primal substance is a throbbing mountain of energy ready and poised to flood through you. You are neither a 'self' responsible for creating this life force, nor a bodyguard protecting your 'self' from it. Inasmuch as your flesh and mind have formerly considered it their solemn duty to own, control, and navigate this tsunami, you need now only open the floodgates of your heart and soul and valiantly allow it. Whereas once your infantile super id feared the immensity of this life force, allowing this white-water rapids to now rip through you, dissolves much of your ego. Your harrowing victim story has always been the single slit straitjacket of human fear. It was once a necessary evil that we can now jettison. As the Buddhists say, you are now capable of Big Love. And as I might add, you are flushed with big gut and soul as well.

And as long as we are dwelling on the fascinating complexities of scientific law, I feel beholden to decipher the purpose of *time* and its indirectly proportional relationship with dark energy and dark matter. At present, science's answer to the question, "Where precisely is dark matter and dark energy?" is roughly, "Duh, we don't know." So for the sake of this interpretation, we will, therefore call all the dark stuff, "invisible stuff." So here goes: the visible yang-expanding universe is a product of time and a function of temporary avoidance of the imperious reality of the nine times as strong yin.

One illuminating definition of time is "that which keeps everything from happening at once." Another telling aspect of time is the differentiation between Isaac Newton's definition of time as a scientifically tangible fourth dimension, versus Emmanuel Kant's description of time as a fundamental man-made artifact with no absolute palpable or measurable attributes of its own. That the first is attributed to a scientist and the second a philosopher, speaks volumes. If we adhere to Kant's philosophical musing, we see the intellect of a human creating a thought form, which helps them to keep everything from happening at once.

But if we saw Newton and Kant's perspectives as both accurate, it might be analogous to imagining the big bang and "God said let there be light" as two equivalent expressions of the same dynamic. If heavy dukkha has always felt impossible for humans to embrace all at once, creating a thought form such as time seems an excellent way to 'divide the sorrow,' so to speak. Science's telescopes look deep out in space and see the past. Out on the edge of space, we see what happened billions of years ago. But we see it *now*. It objectively exists *now*. Let's call it a success, then. The billions of years and light years of what science now calls space/time not only objectively exists as a measurable entity, but it also served its purpose of allowing life to proceed without everything having to have been experienced all at once.

CHAPTER 16

Sane-Pain Child Rearing

Within the biblical admonishment condemning mothers to bear children purportedly to *multiply* their sorrow, is an ossified archetypal riverbed of child rearing. In this dysfunctional, but highly concurred upon template, parents convince themselves and their offspring that Ma and Pa "Johnny on the spot," must leave no stone unturned to have the child circumvent pain at all costs. On its face, protecting children from pain feels like a pretty obvious function that we parents happily provide. What is more insidious, regrettably, is how we parents react to the dukkha (existential pain) that arises from the souls of our children. Since parents, as a rule, presuppose all cries howled from the guts of their children to signify some mechanistic discomfort, we ultimately hypnotize them to likewise overlook their souls as the source of a preponderance of discomposure.

Against this backdrop of expectancy that proclaims we grownups are duty-bound to salve and solve all our children's unease, we open these little ones to the Pandora's box of resentment. Perhaps all souls become incarnate with an archetype of conditional willingness to be a human based solely on God's promise that the butler and maid (Mom and Dad) will mitigate most if not all the pain. This is my belief. But even if this is a ridiculous supposition on my part, like Pavlov's dog, we parents chase our woebegone tails around and around in slavish obedience to the mathematical biblical curse. We obediently multiply our sorrow, not only reflexively reacting to the child's pain with moderate to severe hysteria but also with guilt and insecurity. And of course, the children instinctively sense the flashing neon signs on our furrowed brows that advertise our fear that if we were good parents, our children would not suffer as they do. "Hmmm," they muse, "looks to me like I got me a pair of bozo caretakers. That guilty look on their faces says it all. Seems pretty obvious that if they were good parents, I definitely should not be experiencing this pain. Next time I cry, I won't be emoting just the feeling of objective discomfort; I'll also be including a healthy skosh of subjective, blameful anger to remind the parental book-ends that they are dropping the ball."

Another aspect of the foundationally dysfunctional way parents relate to their child's dukkha concerns the dynamic of how we have so successfully numbed our own pains. Accordingly, when we hear any real agony in the cries of child, our armored musculature and personality quake in genetic harmony. The quaking and shaking of our protected numbness compel us to staunch as best we can the bleating core expression of primordial wounds with which our children objectively were birthed. Between the biblical curse, our Pollyanna ignorant bliss, our hysterical reactions to our children's cries, and our complete and utter insults added to every injury in our lives and theirs, we succeed in providing zero wisdom to how our children might build grace around and through their pains. There'll be no gaining in this paining.

I had a friend once whose young, thoughtlessly aggressive son 'accidentally' smashed his head into her nose. She got a broken nose from his carelessness and immediately began to weep. The child's reaction was to admonish her with his burgeoning self-centeredness: "Why are you crying? I'm the one who's hurt." This woman had previously described her son's less-than-stellar behavior, yet had always resisted my counsel that she deal head-on with his lack of caring. This time, with a very painful face and a quite significant medical bill, she knew it was time to stop her denial of an obvious truth. Though she loved this child with the great, fierce love of primordial motherhood, she just *did not like him much.* What to do now? If and when we dare challenge our child's burgeoning narcissistic attitude that avoiding pain is the core strategy of one's personality, we risk laying bare their suffering to the light of day. Thus exposed, we need not only learn to curb our instinct to rush in and numb them again, but must also curb our guilt that we are the ones peeling the bandage off their wounds.

Four truisms are paramount for parents regarding your child's across-the-board resentment of pain.

1. Drop the BS about children coming in as pure vessels of love and as your teachers. Put on your big boy and big girl pants, and be the damn teachers yourselves. Whether it arose as I suggested before as an archetype supplied by God or is just the little angels' way of assuring us that they indeed intend to multiply our sorrows, too many children assume that their needs are all that exist. If you want this different, you simply *teach* them why that attitude is not good for them, you, the planet, and our species.

2. Ask yourself at what mythical age you assume your child will automatically stop their obsession to hold others responsible for all their pains and treat you like their maid or butler. And remember, this fixation is fueled and reinforced by every demand your child makes for the numbing agents of bad food, bad television, obsessive video games, refusal to participate in the tribal functioning of the family, and the utterance of the devil words, "I'm bored." Sure, it's not enough that you feed your child, clothe him, house him, and tend to every salient need he has; you should be his entertainment guarantor as well.

3. You are going to spend many years tending to your little ones' childhood and countless years afterward parenting them even as they grow into young adulthood. Be freaking honest with yourself. Of course you love them fiercely, and that's awesome; but do you like them nearly as much as your best friend? Even close to that? How much time do you spend making excuses for their behavior? How much time do you spend carping about those who emotionally abuse or disregard you, and yet shy away from holding your beloved child to this same set of standards? And remember this, please: if you who love them can't unequivocally claim to like them, how will they fare in this world with people who do not have unbridled parental love for them? You are their best bet, I promise you.

4. You who vibrantly and genuinely rail against the injustices and inadequacies of our species and our planet have perhaps the greatest duty to sincerely walk your talk. And you who meditate and strive intensely to replace your human foibles with a life of connectedness to some higher consciousness can and must address the fruit that has come from your tree. Just because you love these offspring is zero guarantee that they will become part of the solution and not part of the problem. I call it the curse of Freud—he of the ultra-simplistic pabulum that further encrusts emotional pain as something we are coerced to blame on a parental shortfall of love.

It's a win/win paradigm for sure. While you are challenging your child to stop resenting pain and thereby narcissistically attending almost exclusively to his own comfort, you will be forced to stop numbing and adding insults to your own injuries. All the wisdom and love it will take to truly be the booster rocket launching your child's life toward greatness will be freed in your soul as you work on your own deep-seated misalignments with dukkha.

And last, though I am myself no fan of vaccinations, I have a much bigger beef with the zombie electronics many otherwise-good parents are allowing their children to become hypnotized by. For my money, I believe the precipitous climb in the rate of autism and other childhood cognitive problems are more to do with electronic babysitting than bad food or vaccinations. Very young children are being encouraged to have their early consciousness warped by the sense that all they have to do to engage in life is press buttons. When an adult tries to make actual emotional contact with this small being ... surprise, surprise, the child rebels against the extra effort it takes to be human. Then we bring them to a doctor who ... surprise, surprise, has a diagnosis and a pill. You remember, one pill makes you larger, and one pill makes you small. And when our little angels begin to hit their parents and freak out in other various and sundry ways, we and our doctors can tsk, tsk, tsk that the poor little sweetie has some diagnosable condition that, whew, lets us off the hook that we might otherwise have to work harder teaching our children well. Of course they have an attention deficit—we have allowed them to numb themselves into oblivion, and the effort it will take to get them back will hurt us....and them, ouch.

CHAPTER 17

Knowing Eternity

"We are being sucked into the body of eternity," opines author Terence McKenna about everlasting existence, the often-uttered yet rarely dissected concept. Adds Joseph Campbell, commenting on a Buddhist concept of eternity, "And the attitude of the Bodhicitta is not to withdraw from the world when you realize how horrible it is, but to know that this horror is simply the foreground of a wonder and to come back and participate in it." We already know that yet another author or two (who was that that wrote that ubiquitous thingy called the Bible?) claimed that Christ's sacrifice upon the cross earned him the right to be sucked into the body of eternity. Was the Christ, like the Bodhicitta, willing to suffer thoroughly through the foreground, knowing that eternity in the background would be his (and ostensibly ours) for his effort? And if this unseen place called eternity is one and the same as the unseen stuff called dark matter and dark energy, we might be onto something somewhat fascinating here. And while we're at it, might this unseen place be the same as heaven and home to God, the angels, and the souls of all that have previously tread this land of horror? And lastly, might this unseen place be the realm where imploding X chromosomes first became angry Y chromosomes, who in their hunger for redemption fomented the big bang and the expanding universe we presently prowl?

Nature bequests us even a few more pointers apropos of the eternal cycle of life and death. When a tree in the forest is old and lays down in death, it becomes nutrients upon which a future life will feed. When an animal empties its bowels, that raw material we humans endeavor so hard not to greet with our feet becomes nutrients as well for future life. And when rotten fruit and vegetables become composted, that rot becomes nutrients that will nourish life everlasting. So, while we who measure existence with clocks and calendars turn our noses up at death, shit, and rot, all these 'horrible' signs of life's demise are sucked back into the body of eternity and welcomed as sweet harbingers of a new day. And so it is with the human experience of pain. Just as we react adversely to death, shit, and rot, while nature scoffs at us and uses our "deplorables" to feed eternity, so are our experiences of pain simultaneously deplorable to us and food for the vast body of eternity. Like the Bodhicitta, we are asked not to withdraw from the agonies of this transient existence but to participate in the emulsification of dense engrams into lightened substances that the eternal body feeds upon.

Up to this point, I have lumped all agony into the single notion of dukkha and its direct link to the primordial compression. As we come near the end of this rugged journey out of ignorant bliss and up the Mount Everest of our fully earned tree of knowledge, I bow to the twoness of the one infinite cast of opposites. Night and day, light and dark, cold and hot, happy and sad, woman and man, life and death, yin and yang, the merisms occupy every nook and cranny of our observable and experiential involvement with life. And so the massive remnants of primordial compression that both emerge painfully as Dukkha from our souls, and also reside still magnetically in the core body of eternity, I call the yin female pain. The burning sensation of fiery surrender, as life enters onto death, the light yields itself back into the darkness, and the third Trinitarian gender (the snake) bestows its maleness back into the holy compression, I call the yang male pain.

An ouroboros is an image of a snake swallowing its tail. An iconic painting of a woman holding an hourglass in her hand with this ouroboros floating above her head is one of the universal depictions of eternity. That a woman becomes central to the symbolism connoting time without end is considerably self-evident. Human life eternally flows onward as long as women everlastingly partake in the altruistic transformation of their cells into the building blocks of a new being. So while we automatically pay homage to God for birthing humanity, this sacred enterprise is sustained exclusively through the undying, tender labor of women. In her contractions, the woman is sucked back into the body of eternity. As she enters childbirth (especially for the first time), she realizes how horrible the labor may become, yet like the Bodhicitta, she innately knows that this horror is simply the foreground of the wonder of eternity that she serves.

And while life predominantly falls into the strict dualistic merism of male and female, Eve's Trinitarian ally, the ouroboros, helps describe how and why we are about to end this exploration of pain and purpose with salient cause for an enlightened hope of emergent becoming. Eve's theoretical cuckold, Adam, regularly returns like an angry comet in the night, with the patriarchal male lie that follows him through history as tail and tale of the fiery orb. But an aspect of maleness embodied in the snake rejects the spiteful way Adam has forgotten from whence he came, and worse, *why* he came. The snake, the ouroboros, knew Eve and knows woman still. It swallows its tail and represents infinity because, in the end, it returns itself to Eve, following the script the Infinite has designed. The end of the journey for the ouroboros is back in the womb of the primordial compression, and back in the soul/genitals of Eve. The ouroboros returns to the membrane separating primal X queen's purely female domain, and the imploded inner space where Y's momentarily reside before bursting never-endingly into this expanding cosmos. So whereas the female has up to now had to primarily rely purely on banging angry Y's to pierce her density, the second coming of the snake promises that this evolving maleness will swallow its tail and humbly give itself to the opening of the Queen's need. Just as death begets new life, the ouroboros devours itself and ends its male linear journey through time so the eternal female can be released from her black hole density in a rebirth of humanity.

For those of us men who are repulsed by the nagging patriarchal remnants still percolating in crevices of our souls, the ouroboros offers us hope that an emergent sacred masculine is more than a hip new-age cliché. Just as Hawking's radiation is yang light that no longer needs to fear the nine times as powerful darkness that has swallowed it, there is an endarkened path toward hallowed cosmic duty for men who seek it.

Chapter 18

And in the End

Bearing in mind the incalculable wealth of knowledge that has been luminously unearthed by both science and philosophy, it is striking that the phenomenological dominion of pain has remained so vastly under-scrutinized. As nature abhors a vacuum, in this intellectual paucity where the objective ache is so minimally comprehended, the insults we add to our injuries have held sway. Whether or not my effort to broach this abyss has infused you with conceivable alternatives to self-insult, I trust, at least, that you'll meet your self-invectives with a bit more nuanced listening.

And thus, to begin subtracting insults from your injuries, you need not be entirely convinced of my theory. There is an expression in the Cooper clan that "we shoot for the stars, and if we fall short, we at least make it to the moon." So if I failed to persuade you of the universe's indebtedness to you for your forbearance of agony, yet have furnished you even a trifling sense to initiate subtracting unwarranted affronts to your hurting, we will rejoice in the lunar landscape together.

While we all tend toward human identification and egoistic individuation, we are in fact comprised *only* of objective universal materials. So whereas I picture myself as Alan, accustomed to the predictability of Alan's feelings and thoughts, beneath the façade of this 'me', lies all the holographic energies that govern the entire cosmos. So when my or your prefrontal cortex dumps archetypal cynical explanations on us for why one pain or another is happening at the moment, let's clear our throats and declare, "Ahem, I beg to differ." When the long-distance runner hits the wall at about twenty miles, and her mind screams, "Stop running! I'm dying. My legs can't take it anymore," another voice inside her knows better and instead wins the day. She keeps dashing and reaches the runner's high, endorphins cheering her on with unabashed ardor. She finishes the race and experiences the splendid, immediate rewards of subtracting insult from injury. Synchronously, just as the runner has, a sane voice in your mind is screaming for you to likewise triumphantly override your outdated cerebral nattering negativity.

In closing, *Subtracting Insult from Injury* is a handbook for a most challenging slice of the human experience. Our agonies, my dear friends, are not only the elephant in the room; they are the room itself. While animals might be content, never grasping the whys and wherefores of their immediate suffering, inquiring human minds demand coherent ammunition against the fickle quirks of the unknown. And whether the shape of this logical rejoinder to every single pain presents itself in the form of guilt, blame, fear, self-doubt, or utter existential resentment of God's ways, the insults that we routinely add to our injuries have I hope been somewhat laid bare by the scrutiny of this book. Ideally, you have become even slightly more empowered to recognize and self-edit the daily robotic, deleterious mental editorializing that accompanies your angsts, small or large. You have updated the hard drive of your subconscious relationship to all of your past traumas, small and large. Pulling back the cosmic veil of mystery, you have explored how and why a species of rational beings would create a myth (or channel a Bible) in which their God would vehemently forbid them the truth. We have opened a door for you to pose questions such as: What could be so verboten that by knowing it, we became eternal 'sinners'? And how was the disease of blaming Eve for 'the fall' plumbed out of the collective vision? I trust that your continuing pilgrimage to answer these questions will aid you in transforming yourself from a slave of pain into its master.

In Romans 8:22, Paul states, "From the beginning until now, the entire creation as we know it has been groaning in one great act of giving birth."

In 1999, my boundless former wife, our eight children, and I rather incongruously ended up living in Kosovo (former Yugoslavia), where a horrific ethnic cleansing at the hands of Slobodan Milosevic had just transpired. Instead of a month of do-gooding in refugee camps that I initially foresaw as a possibility, we remained there for over four years. To this day, each time I am asked why we went in the first place, I dig deeper inside for a more profoundly sincere response. This is because I truly can't quite yet answer the question with total authenticity. I do not presently live my life in the unqualified relinquishment of self that swept the ten of us into what we called in those days "the undertow of hearts."

Looking back through the lens of wonderment at the past, there was a cryptic alchemy that developed between us and the liberated souls of these Kosovars. *Liberated?* I'm calling victims whose family members had been ripped from their arms and massacred, *liberated*? Indeed, for Kosovars had been virtually stripped and liberated from the Pollyanna platitudes of Western thought. Like a tree adores the carbon dioxide we humans consider a toxic byproduct of our respiration, and we adore the oxygenated waste product of theirs, we Coopers fell madly in love with the rarified grace that emanated from these Kosovars. They likewise seemed to grok us, as no Americans had heretofore experienced. As I have often stressed in this book, there are two ways to have pain end. One is to numb it, and one is to alchemize and heal it. The grace we experienced from an overwhelming swath of the Kosovar populace was a living, breathing embodiment of raw, un-numbed pain and the way it vibrates in holy concert with God's design. And bypassing any false modesty as to how we Coopers figured in this alchemy of pain, perhaps our quantum beholding of the Kosovars' beauty was a treasured piece of the puzzle.

Abel, the youngest of our eight, was six years old when we moved to Kosovo. He and the entire family learned the Kosovar dialect of the Albanian language. Sally worked brilliantly with a whole village of widows whose husbands had all been rounded up and massacred by Serb paramilitaries in Qyshk on May 14, 1999. Our three eldest, Casey Katie, and Sophie, volunteered tirelessly with Balkan Sunflowers, an NGO dedicated to Kosovo's children who had witnessed far too much horror. The five younger children (Will ,Cloee, Cicily, Ariel, and Abel) innately became an un-definable substance that met the raw mass PTSD of the Kosovars with what appeared as effortless fluency. I wrote two plays, which starred members of Kosovo's national theatre, our children, and some of the widows of Qyshk. Both theatre pieces were allegorical and paid homage to how the Kosovars emerged with an incomprehensibly powerful collective grace from their ethnic cleansing. The second play was performed in Athens when the Olympic Games auspiciously returned there in 2004. The following emails arose in reaction to our family's work and commitment to healing and peace in the Balkans, which culminated during what was called Olympic Truce Week in the days before the Athens Games commenced.

Dear Cooper family, our warm greetings.

To you and the people of Kosovo who have come to Greece for Olympic Truce Week to witness for peace, and the gracious

Greek people who have received you. I salute your efforts to promote peace and reconciliation on the behalf of humanity.

God bless you,
Desmond Tutu, Archbishop Emeritus

Dear Dr. Alan and Sally Cooper,

The private secretary of HM King Constantine has kindly authorized us to arrange a meeting for you with HRH Princess Irene of Greece. She is very much looking forward to the joy and privilege of meeting people such as yourselves, dedicated to the quest for peace, who inspire our entire admiration and respect. You are an example for all humanity.

With Kindest Regards,
World in Harmony, Madrid

While I am eternally gratified for this feedback we received in reaction to our time in Kosovo, it is nothing compared with the vast pride I feel for the people there. Let me share just one of countless examples of the Kosovar spirit. All of the five grown sons of Mihane Lushi lived with their wives and children in the village of Qyshk. On that day, May 14th, the five of them were amongst the men of the village that were massacred. There would be no 'Saving Private Ryan' happy ending for Mihane Lushi. All five of her sons robustly awoke that morning yet were dead by sun-down. When we met this woman, just months after the massacre, she had an otherworldly purport to her every movement, like plaintive graceful poetry in motion.

For the first few years in Kosovo all our efforts had been exclusively on behalf of The Albanian Kosovar victims of Milosevic. Then, out of nowhere, Sally and I were asked one day to give a closing speech the following week at a groundbreaking gathering of teens and young adults that included Serbs as well as Albanians. We felt moved to participate, but couldn't hardly comprehend how some of the Albanians we loved so much would react to us interacting with Serbs who they still feared and resented so greatly. There was but one way for us to decide, and we went and asked Mihane if she felt we should do it or not. The decision would be entirely hers. In the Grand Canyon that had been carved in her gut/soul by a cruel fate, Mihane took the question in and paused majestically. Then like an eagle, her auric wings parted and she spoke. "When my children were young they always played with the Serbian children and never had any problems. They all loved each other. Those young Serbs you will talk in front of are innocent. I want the children to be able to play together again. Please, go do your talk."

Ryve Lushi, one of Mihane's five widowed daughters-in-law, starred as herself in both of our plays. Like her transcendent mother-in-law, Ryve can barely be described in words that are used for human beings. I won't try. Fatos Lajci, who epitomizes so much of the coal under pressure diamonds carved in the Kosovar collective soul, was our blindfolded guide and an angel without artifice or affect.

I leave you with a poem I wrote some decades ago.

No Chair in Paradise

Once upon a time, behind the sublime mystery of the divine line that marks the point where gods combine, less than a truce was struck between the old and the new.

Less than a sigh was voiced, and hardly a matter of martyred truth was viewed without being construed as lewd, as a matter of fancy or fact.

And though the lure of these words starts out absurd, obscuring deeper cries from being heard, they begin their flight winged, I having begged a bird for sanctuary.

But lest you wilt before my stare, my mind, my ugly sneering dare, you should be warned about the place where emptiness has stolen care and rendered husky-throated entreaties bare.

Now a common enemy, two-headed, mask-less, there to see, defines, refines, confines really this maudlin play of history.

Where once the two stood face-to-face, discordant duets mocked our race, the laugh-less joke was much too base, disgrace in place of vision.

Not once did our tears run about, where pebbles even marked a route, or orphans often even shout, "My pain is real. I have no doubt."

The tragedy is all the more. No villain here has fixed this score, no bloodstained coins have paid the whore, high-stepping boots kicked down no door, and bottles sucked up on the shore say, "Shipwrecked ain't against the law."

So two or more back bound as one. Alas the beached whale's death-dance done. I know a few who'd pay a ton to hear this isn't so.

For even those who play to win would sooner lose than dare begin, to sink down where we're all akin to empty depths where whales have been.

And advertised upon that fin that once held life (at least life's twin), a truth found in God's garbage bin, the holy sounds, a dirge-like din: "Eternity's been strained?"

For larger than the world of light that nobly watches o'er the night, and even bigger than the pains the anguished world of dark contains, are vacuumed voids where deafness reigns.

To contact me with any questions or reactions, email miraclestruggle@gmail.com

Finisimo

Made in the USA
Las Vegas, NV
29 November 2021